BEST LOVED GARDEN PLANTS

BEST LOVED
GARDEN PLANTS

DAVID MYERS • LANCE HATTATT • LINDSAY BOUSFIELD

Illustrations by
ELAINE FRANKS

This edition first published in 1996 by
Parragon
13 Whiteladies Road
Clifton
Bristol BS8 1PB

Reprinted 1998

Produced by
Robert Ditchfield Ltd
Combe Court, Kerry's Gate
Hereford HR2 0AH

ISBN 0 75252 557 3

A copy of the British Library Cataloguing in Publication Data is available from the Library.

Typeset by Action Typesetting Ltd, Gloucester
Colour origination by Mandarin Offset Ltd, Hong Kong
Printed and bound in Italy

ACKNOWLEDGEMENTS

Many of the photographs were taken in the authors' gardens and nurseries at Bromesberrow Place (David Myers),
Arrow Cottage, Ledgemoor, Weobley (Lance Hattatt) and Acton Beauchamp Roses, Worcester (Lindsay Bousfield).
The publishers would also like to thank the many people and organizations who have allowed photographs to be taken
for this book, including the following:

Mr and Mrs Terence Aggett; Lucinda Aldrich-Blake; Polly Bolton, Nordybank Nurseries, Clee St Margaret; Burford
House, Tenbury Wells; Lallie Cox, Woodpeckers, Marlcliff, Bidford-on-Avon; Mr and Mrs K. Dawson, Chennels Gate,
Eardisley; Dinmore Manor; Richard Edwards, Well Cottage, Blakemere; Great Dixter; Haseley Court; Hatsford
Fuchsias; The Hon Mrs Peter Healing, The Priory, Kemerton; Hereford City Parks Department; Hergest Croft; Mrs
Daphne Hoskins, Kellaways; Mrs R. Humphries, Orchard Bungalow, Bishops Frome; Mr and Mrs J. James; Mrs David
Lewis, Ash Farm, Much Birch; Mottisfont Abbey (National Trust); Mr and Mrs R. Norman; Mrs Richard Paice, Bourton
House; Pentwyn Cottage Garden, Bacton; The Picton Garden, Colwall; Powis Castle (National Trust); Mrs Clive
Richards, Lower Hope, Ullingswick; Mary Anne Robinson; Royal Botanic Gardens, Kew; RHS Garden, Wisley;
Sissinghurst Castle (National Trust); Stone House Cottage, Kidderminster; Raymond Treasure, Stockton Bury Farm,
Kimbolton; Wakehurst Place (National Trust); Richard Walker; Mr and Mrs S de R Wall; Mrs Geoffrey Williams, Close
Farm, Crockham Hill; Mr and Mrs R. Williams; Mrs David Williams-Thomas, The Manor House, Birlingham; Wyevale
Garden Centre, Hereford; York Gate, Leeds.

Photographs of the following plants are reproduced by kind permission of Thompson & Morgan Ltd., Ipswich, Suffolk;
Salvia splendens, Sweet Pea 'Maggie May', 'Snoopea' and 'Cupid Mixed'.

Photographs of the following roses are reproduced by kind permission of Mattocks Roses (Notcutts, Woodbridge,
Suffolk): 'City Lights', 'Perestroika', 'Queen Mother', 'Regensburg', 'Royal William', 'Scarlet Patio', 'Simba', 'Valois Rose'.

Photographs of the following roses are reproduced by kind permission of Lindsay Bousfield: Compassion, Hermosa,
Irene Watts, Leverkusen, Perle d'Or, Sombreuil.

CONTENTS

HOW TO USE THIS BOOK

Where appropriate, approximate measurements of a plant's height have been given, and also the spread where this is significant, in both metric and imperial measures. The height is the first measurement, as for example 1.2m × 60cm/4 × 2ft. However, both height and spread vary so greatly from garden to garden since they depend on soil, climate and position, that these measurements are offered as guides only. This is especially true of trees and shrubs where ultimate growth can be unpredictable.

The following symbols are also used throughout the book:
  ○ = thrives best or only in full sun
  ◑ = thrives best or only in part-shade
  ● = succeeds in full shade
  E = evergreen
  H = Frost hardy down to 5°C (23°F)
Where no sun symbol and no reference to sun or shade is made in the text, it can be assumed that the plant tolerates sun or light shade.

PLANT NAMES

For ease of reference this book gives the botanical name under which a plant is most widely listed for the gardener. These names are sometimes changed and in such cases the new name has been included. Common names are given wherever they are in frequent use.

POISONOUS PLANTS

In recent years, concern has been voiced about poisonous plants or plants which can cause allergic reactions if touched. The fact is that many plants are poisonous, some in a particular part, others in all their parts. For the sake of safety, it is always, without exception, essential to assume that no part of a plant should be eaten unless it is known, without any doubt whatsoever, that the plant or its part is edible and that it cannot provoke an allergic reaction in the individual person who samples it. It must also be remembered that some plants can cause severe dermatitis, blistering or an allergic reaction if touched, in some individuals and not in others. It is the responsibility of the individual to take all the above into account.

FUCHSIAS

FUCHSIAS HAVE BECOME IMMENSELY POPULAR in
recent years. This is probably due to the wide
colour range and exotic shapes of the flowers,
together with their relative ease of cultivation.
They also provide colour in the garden over a
long period, from midsummer to late
autumn. These qualities make them particularly valuable in the modern small garden.

Hardy varieties are especially useful for
brightening rock gardens and shrub borders,
after most of the other residents have ceased
blooming. Half-hardy types are mainly planted in hanging baskets or containers and are
grown outside from early summer until
autumn, when they are returned to the greenhouse. Standard types are also bedded out
after the risk of frost has diminished.

Varieties with small to medium sized
blooms generally produce the best continuous displays and tolerate wet weather conditions better than large double-flowered types.
These often prove to be shyer in flower production and may require the protection of the
greenhouse to attain perfection.

PLANNING YOUR DISPLAY
The initial step is to co-ordinate the colour
scheme of your display. Personal preference
will determine whether you opt for strong

Fuchsia 'Thalia' in a sea of nasturtiums.

Plants in a wall-pot give the effect of a cascade.

colours or subtle pastel shades. The colour and texture of the backgrounds which are to support your arrangements need to be considered, to make sure that the flowers create a suitable contrast.

I always advocate experimenting with something new, as this provides a challenge, together with a sense of anticipation, in the garden. Fuchsias can produce stunning displays, both on their own, or when grown with other compatible plants. In either case suitable varieties need to be chosen to produce harmonious displays when in bloom. Growth habits and eventual heights must be taken into consideration.

Summer displays in conservatories can be enhanced by fuchsias in hanging baskets and pots. It is essential, however, that ventilation and shading are available to offset high temperatures in periods of strong sunlight.

Fuchsias prove unsatisfactory in the house unless positioned in a very light window. Insufficient natural light results in premature flower drop.

A gardener with imagination will find there are many ways to display fuchsias in the garden. Walls, pillars, posts and fences can be festooned with hanging baskets; patios, porches and drives bedecked with containers of all kinds.

PROPAGATION

Stock plants or 'Mother Plants' provide the shoots from which cuttings for propagation are taken. Cuttings can be taken during spring and summer, selecting non-flowering shoots with two pairs of leaves. Remove the

A fine standard fuchsia tones with impatiens at its feet.

A barrel of pendulous fuchsias and begonias gives a long display.

lower pair, apply rooting hormone to the base of the cutting and insert to a depth of 2cm/1in in seed compost with perlite or sand incorporated. The tray or pot is then watered and placed in a shaded situation, preferably in a propagator in the glasshouse or on the window-sill, where rooting should occur within fourteen days.

CARE AND CULTIVATION

Once they are well rooted, transfer the cuttings to 9cm/3½in pots. A proprietary peat potting compost, or soil-based John Innes no. 2, provide a suitable growing medium. Insert them to the same depth, lightly firm in and water. Now is the time they thrive on warmth, 15°C/60°F minimum if possible, until they become established. Watering is required whenever the compost becomes fairly dry. In order to produce a bush fuchsia, pinch out the growing tip above three pairs of leaves. If a standard is required leave it to grow on.

Eventually, when the plant becomes 'pot bound' and the roots emerge through the base of the pot, it will need transferring to a larger container. This could take the form of a hanging basket, or receptacle in the greenhouse or outside. The same compost may be used for replanting.

Lilium 'Pink Perfection', fuchsia and nemesia.

When positioning your fuchsias in the garden, it is most important to guard against the plants becoming 'cooked' during periods of hot sunny weather. 'Dappled shade' is what they crave outside, shaded greenhouses if they are grown inside.

During the summer, regular watering and liquid feeding is necessary, whenever the plants begin to show signs of wilting. Fertilizer containing nitrogen and potash in equal proportions is ideal.

PESTS AND DISEASES

Fuchsias, like many other plants, act as hosts to various insects and fungi.

APHIDS (Greenfly)

These make their presence known as white scaly skins situated on the upper surfaces of the leaves below the growing tip. They have been discarded by the aphids living on the underside of the leaves just above. Control with a proprietary aphid spray.

WHITEFLY

These reside on the underside of leaves especially just below the growing tip. The adults fly off when you shake the plant. The worst legacy of this pest is the black sooty mould, which grows on the sugary secretion exuded by the insects. This defaces the plant's appearance. Control with a proprietary spray.

VINE WEEVIL

The larvae of this elusive beetle are located in the soil. They are cream coloured, up to 1cm/½in long, with chestnut brown heads. They merrily chomp through the roots of your plants, causing them to wilt and eventually die. Dispose of grubs and affected soil.

Fuchsia 'Mrs Popple' is wonderfully floriferous and has the added merit of being frost-hardy.

BOTRYTIS (Grey mould)

Grey spores grow on dead or damaged plant tissue which can spread to healthy leaves and flowers. It is necessary to reduce humidity within the environment by adequate ventilation of the greenhouse and careful watering during wet weather.

FUCHSIA RUST

This shows as light green patches on the upper surfaces of leaves, which, when inspected from below, reveal rusty brown areas of spores. Reducing humidity deters this problem and also affected leaves can be removed and destroyed.

13

1. FUCHSIAS FOR HANGING BASKETS

Fuchsias are the ideal plants for baskets, which give their pendant blooms the best possible display.

PLANTING *a* BASKET

THE HABIT OF GROWTH of a large proportion of fuchsia varieties determines that their flowers are allowed to cascade downwards in mid-air. Hence the practice of growing them in pots and baskets suspended aloft, where the true beauty of the flowers can be appreciated.

1. Make up baskets in the greenhouse during early spring when plants are available.

2. Wire baskets require lining with moss or a proprietary liner in order to contain the compost.

3. 'Pinched', well-branched plants of pendulous or arching varieties, should be used. Five plants in a 35cm/14in diameter basket produce an excellent display.

4. Fill the basket with 'John Innes' or peat compost, to within 10cm/4in of the rim. Place the plants around the edge angling them outwards, with one in the centre if space allows. Firm around with compost, leaving an indentation for watering.

5. Hang in the greenhouse or place on a large pot and water thoroughly. They should be kept here until early summer, and watered whenever the compost becomes dry.

Wire baskets, galvanized or plastic-coated, suspended by chains, are the traditional types of container. Plastic hanging pots, which do not require lining with moss, have become popular and are available in a range of styles and colours. Where space is restricted half-baskets of wire or plastic can be fixed flush against the wall.

PLANTING *a* BASKET

SITING

It is important to guard against fuchsias becoming 'cooked' during hot weather. They crave dappled shade in which to thrive. A sunny aspect should therefore be avoided.

MAINTENANCE

Daily watering is normally required, except during wet weather when it should be withheld.

A balanced liquid feed of equal parts nitrogen and potash is essential for sustained flowering of your basket.

17

1. **'Cascade'** A free-branching pendulous variety with medium-sized flowers. Sepals are white, flushed rose-pink; the corolla is rose.

2. **'Harry Gray'** A double-flowered, compact, self-branching trailer. Sepals are white with pink veins; corolla white, pink at the base.

3. **'Autumnale'** A strong-growing trailer with red-bronze foliage. The single flowers have red sepals and rose red corolla.

4. **'Jack Shahan'** Single, large-flowered pendulous variety with pale pink sepals and a rose corolla. The growth is robust.

5. **'La Campanella'** Profuse semi-double flowers on a compact, freely branching trailer. Small flowers with white sepals (tinged pink) and a mauve corolla.

The **corolla** is the tube of petals around the centre of the fuchsia. The **sepals** are the outer 'skirt'.

5.

'Swingtime' A vigorous, large-flowered double with arching growth. Shiny deep pink sepals, white pink-veined corolla.

'Brutus' is a vigorous, floriferous, single hardy, with red sepals and deep purple corolla.

'Mrs Churchill' Semi-vigorous, single-flowered, lax-growing variety.

◆ *Difficult to grow because of its shy-branching habit.*

FUCHSIAS *for* HANGING BASKETS

'Marinka' A vigorous, floriferous, single-flowered variety, with a cascading habit of growth. Sepals shiny red with darker red corolla.

'Annabel' Strong-growing, double, upright loose bush. Medium-sized flowers, sepals white tinged pink, corolla white with pink veins.

'Coachman' Vigorous single, with an arching habit. Flowers medium-sized with salmon sepals and glowing orange corolla.

'Beacon Rosa' Extremely free-flowering, moderate-growing single, with upright habit, though arching when it flowers. Sepals bright pink with pink corolla.

◆ *This variety is often considered to be hardy.*

'Blue Satin' Large-flowered double, with white sepals and dark mauve corolla, white at base. Moderate arching growth.

'Leonora' Vigorous, free-flowering single. Medium-sized blooms have salmon-pink sepals and rose corolla. Growth upright and arching.

'Frosted Flame' Early-flowering single with pendulous growth. Sepals white, green tipped with pink inside, and long corolla.

◆ *Shy branching variety. Pinch out the side shoots several times.*

'Flying Cloud' Sturdy double, producing upright arching growth. Sepals white flushed pink, corolla white with pink veins at the base.

FUCHSIAS CAN ALSO BE USED TO GREAT EFFECT when incorporated with other types of plants, such as pelargoniums, petunias, lobelia etc., to produce a mixed hanging basket. The ultimate reward for all your efforts comes when you are able to relax on a warm summer's evening, watching the swinging blooms overhead.

'Red Spider' Prolific single with long crimson sepals and deep rose-pink veined corolla. Moderate growth, extremely pendulous.

◆ *Excellent variety for edges of containers and baskets.*

'Rose of Denmark' Semi-double with arching and pendulous habit. Medium-sized blooms.

'White Spider' Vigorous single with long pink sepals and white pink-veined corolla. Growth loose, long and arching.

'Pink Galore' Attractive, shy-branching double, of medium vigour and pendulous habit.

◆ *Ideal to cascade down the front of a pot or basket.*

'Miss California' Early-flowering semi-double with long pale pink sepals and white pink-veined corolla. Thin-stemmed upright, arching habit.

'Pink Galore' provides colour around the base of this basket by cascading below the other flowers.

◆ *The grey helichrysum presents an ideal contrasting background.*

'Display' Extremely free-flowering, single, hardy variety with bushy habit. It has pink sepals and a deep rose corolla.

'Border Queen' Free-branching single. Sepals are pale pink, tipped green, the corolla violet, veined pink.

WATERING FUCHSIAS IN A HANGING BASKET every day can be demanding on the gardener, especially if he has several to maintain. If they are on a house wall, they can sometimes be soaked from within by leaning out of a window. Otherwise, install a permanent micro-irrigation system which will water the basket at the turn of a tap.

FUCHSIAS *for* HANGING BASKETS

Three separate varieties of fuchsia are planted in this 20cm/8in hanging pot. They are the double white-flowered **'Annabel'**, single pink-flowered **'Leonora'** and single mauve and white **'Border Queen'**.

◆ *Each of these varieties produces upright and arching growth, making them a compatible combination.*

2. Fuchsias for Containers

Fuchsias are extremely versatile plants for containers. Arching varieties decorate hard, unattractive edges, whilst upright and standard types provide the extra dimension of height.

UPRIGHT FUCHSIAS

IN LARGER CONTAINERS, a variety with an upright habit is required for the centre where it provides the necessary height. For this purpose, a half-standard fuchsia is excellent, as it produces a two-tiered effect. In full bloom it will give a dramatic extended display. Such plants are especially welcome beside a garden seat where one can admire the delicacy of the flowers.

1.

1. **'Joy Patmore'** Bushy upright growing single, having masses of medium-sized flowers. Sepals pure white recurving, corolla deep rose-pink.
2. **'Jack Acland'** Strong upright free-flowering single. Medium-sized flowers having pink sepals and dark rose corolla fading to reddish-rose.
3. **'Estelle Marie'** Strong free-branching upright single, with medium-sized flowers held erect. Sepals white with green tips. Corolla violet, white at base.
4. **'Celia Smedley'** Vigorous growing, shy-branching, large single flowered upright. Sepals white tinged rose, corolla vivid scarlet.
5. **'Cloverdale Pearl'** Self-branching bushy single, producing an abundance of medium-sized flowers. Sepals pink fading to white, corolla tubular and white.

Upright varieties are ideal as a focal point in the centre of containers to provide height to the arrangement.

Many upright growers develop an arching habit due to the weight of the maturing blooms. This must be considered when positioning in the container.

UPRIGHT FUCHSIAS

Upright varieties should always be selected when planting in borders so that the flowers are clear of the soil.

'Thalia' (Triphylla type) Vigorous upright, late-flowering variety. Bright orange-scarlet blooms, freely produced.

'Rufus the Red' (H) Vigorous upright bush, producing medium-sized single flowers in profusion.

'Prodigy' (H) Strong-growing upright with medium-sized semi-double flowers. Bright red sepals, rich purple-pink corolla.

'Snowcap' (H) Upright bush with semi-double flowers. Sepals are bright red and shiny. White corolla, pink-veined at base.

'Dawn' Upright bush carrying masses of medium-sized single blooms. White-tipped green sepals, mauve-blue corolla, paler at base.

'Marin Glow' Upright, free-flowering single. Medium-sized blooms. Pure white sepals and deep purple tubular corollas.

'Lye's Unique' Very vigorous upright growth, freely producing medium-sized, slender tubular flowers.

'Lilian Lampard' Vigorous self-branching upright with medium-sized blooms freely produced. White sepals with pink-lilac, tubular corolla.

'Royal Velvet' Large double. An upright bushy grower with deep pink sepals and dark purple corolla streaked crimson.

'Swanley Gem' Upright single. Medium-sized flowers having recurved scarlet sepals with mauve scarlet-veined corolla.

'Morning Glow' Upright bush, producing medium-sized, semi-double blooms freely. Pale pink recurved sepals, lilac corolla.

UPRIGHT FUCHSIAS

When growing large-flowered types, an aspect sheltered from the wind is essential to avoid flower damage.

'Gypsy Queen' Upright, large double free-flowering bush, with swept-back red sepals and a mauve corolla.

'Mieke Meursing' (H) Compact, floriferous single. Upright with medium-sized blooms. Red sepals and pink veined corolla.

'Dollar Princess' (H) Bushy, upright double. The stems arch on flowering. Cerise sepals with rich purple corolla.

'Garden News' (H) Shy-branching upright with semi-double flowers. Sepals reluctant to recurve.

'Tennessee Waltz' (H) Upright and arching habit, with double flowers. Pink sepals and lavender rose-streaked corolla.

29

SPREADING FUCHSIAS

VARIETIES WITH AN ARCHING HABIT OF GROWTH are ideal for planting around the edges of the containers so that the flowers cascade down in front of them. In all cases, the containers have to be deep enough to allow the pendulous flowers of a mature plant to droop without trailing onto the ground.

'Quaser' Large double free-flowered trailing variety with white sepals and full pinkish-lilac corolla streaked white at base.

'Eva Boerg' Early-flowering semi-double with pale pink sepals and purple corolla, splashed pink at base.

'Gay Paree' Medium-sized double-flowering trailer. Reflexed pale pink sepals; the corolla is mottled with shades of pink and purple.

'Dark Eyes' Upright bushy grower producing medium-sized double blooms. Shiny deep red sepals, violet-blue corolla, rose at base.

'Annabel' Strong-growing medium-sized double with upright arching growth.

'Vanessa Jackson' Large single-flowered trailer. Flared salmon-orange sepals. Rose-red corolla streaked salmon-orange at base.

'Muriel' Profuse, large-flowering single with vigorous, cascading habit. Scarlet sepals, pale purple-veined rose corolla.

'Leverhulme' (Triphylla type) Vigorous upright free-flowering variety. Deep glowing-pink sepals and corolla.

'Enchanted' A prolific large double. Rose-red sepals with mauve corolla, streaked pink.

'Brutus' (H) Early-flowering single with deep pink sepals and dark purple corolla. Thin-stemmed, arching growth.

'Gartenmeister Bonstedt' (Triphylla type) Late variety with dark foliage, veined red-bronze. Bright orange sepals and corolla.

'Dancing Flame' Double with arching habit. Orange sepals, orange-carmine corolla, streaked lighter orange at base.

'Sunny Smiles' Large blooming single with arching growth which trails. Pale salmon-pink sepals, crimson corolla with paler base.

'Beacon' Strong-growing upright bush which arches in flower. Medium-sized single flowers with scarlet sepals and mauvish scarlet-veined corolla.

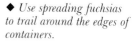

◆ *Use spreading fuchsias to trail around the edges of containers.*

31

CONTAINER DISPLAYS

POTS, TUBS AND TROUGHS are traditionally used as containers. However, old wheelbarrows, chimney pots, hollow logs or anything which holds sufficient compost to grow the plants, is suitable. Often these are placed on pedestals to enhance the display of the blooms, which only reveal their true beauty when viewed from below.

Fuchsias can be planted in association with a large variety of plants, to produce mixed displays.

Fuchsias can be grown in pots and subsequently placed close together to produce a solid bed of flowers.

'Thalia'

'Waveney Gem'

Nowadays, it has become customary to arrange these containers on patios amid the confusion of toys, furniture and barbeques, where children glean constant pleasure from 'popping' the bauble-shaped buds dripping in front of them.

Pelargoniums, lobelia, alyssum and busy lizzies were traditionally used with fuchsias, but recently people have become more adventurous with osteospermums, diascias, felicias etc.

In this arrangement of pots, the fuchsia flowers add extra variety and form to the coloured foliage of the coleus.

'Elfriede Ott'

'Olive Moon'

3. STANDARD FUCHSIAS

A very popular way of growing fuchsias is as standards. These forms can provide the gardener with really eye-catching displays.

TRAINING *a* STANDARD FUCHSIA

STANDARD FUCHSIAS or 'tree fuchsias' as they are often called, are grown so that the flowers are held high above the ground, where they are displayed to perfection. It is essential to choose varieties which are self-branching and produce flowers freely. They should also have an upright arching habit of growth to form a round head.

The rooted cutting is potted into a 10cm/4in pot during the spring and is left unstopped.

The plant is trained to a cane as it grows and flower buds are removed as they appear.

It is important that side shoots are present in the axils of at least four pairs of leaves before stopping.

The growing-tip is pinched out when the desired height is reached. This is usually at least 1m/3ft.

Once stopped, the side shoots quickly develop. The growing points should be pinched out after two pairs of leaves are present.

The head of a mature standard in spring (*left*) showing new shoots being produced on existing wooden branches.

The tips of the shoots are removed (*right*) to produce a rounded head and encourage the growth of additional side shoots.

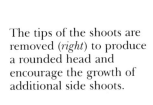

TRAINING *a* STANDARD FUCHSIA

'Royal Velvet' creates a magnificent display of sumptuous, large blooms, shown to perfection.

This head is adequately clothed with sufficient shoots to generate a good, shapely display of flowers.

Repotting into a slightly larger pot should take place each time the compost becomes thoroughly filled with roots.

Water the plants whenever they become dry and begin to wilt.

Liquid-feeding, using a balanced fertilizer, enhances the performance of the plant once it begins to flower.

Check that the cane support is adequate and secure the plant to it as your standard develops.

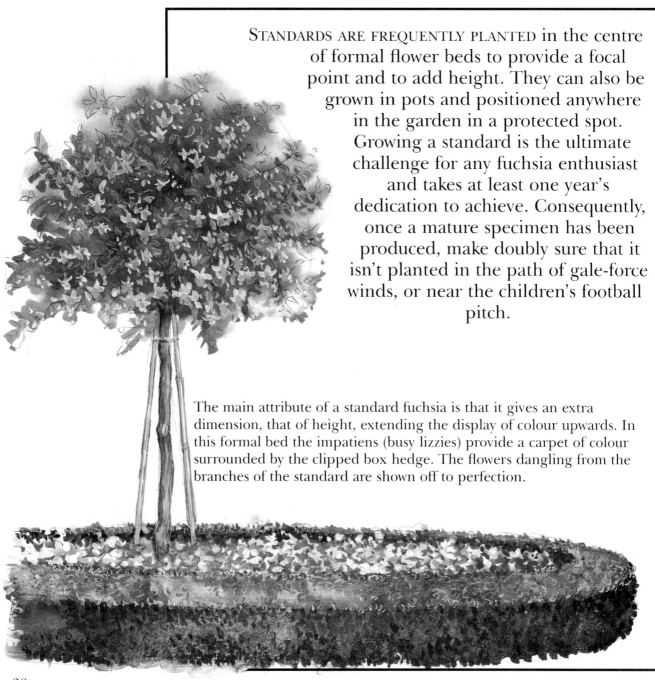

STANDARDS ARE FREQUENTLY PLANTED in the centre of formal flower beds to provide a focal point and to add height. They can also be grown in pots and positioned anywhere in the garden in a protected spot. Growing a standard is the ultimate challenge for any fuchsia enthusiast and takes at least one year's dedication to achieve. Consequently, once a mature specimen has been produced, make doubly sure that it isn't planted in the path of gale-force winds, or near the children's football pitch.

The main attribute of a standard fuchsia is that it gives an extra dimension, that of height, extending the display of colour upwards. In this formal bed the impatiens (busy lizzies) provide a carpet of colour surrounded by the clipped box hedge. The flowers dangling from the branches of the standard are shown off to perfection.

The bright pink-flowered standard adds height to the display of containers whilst extending the range of the pink colour scheme.

This standard serves to provide a pinnacle of colour and marks the position of steps to a higher garden.

An imposing display is created by positioning standards beside the entrance to one's house.

Plain areas of the garden can be instantly enlivened by the introduction of a standard grown in a pot.

A 'false' standard of a basket on a pole breaks up an expanse of patio.

Standards can be usefully placed to supply additional islands of colour and interest in established herbaceous borders.

A standard triphylla produces a focal point in a small bed and contrasts beautifully with yellow nasturtiums.

SITING *a* STANDARD FUCHSIA

A standard fuchsia has been aptly chosen to give height in a narrow bed beside a house wall.

◆ *It rises from a sea of harmoniously coloured nicotianas.*

'Border Queen' Strong free-branching single producing an abundance of medium-sized blooms.

The impressive effect of grouping standards whereby they form a wall round part of a garden.

◆ *Note that they have been arranged to take account of differing heights.*

'Devonshire Dumpling' Strong, compact, free-branching, arching growth bearing plump double flowers.

'Miss California' Early-flowering semi-double. Thin-stemmed, arching growth.

Both height and colour are brought to a border by a standard.

Tall fuchsias, arranged according to height, cascade forwards.

A fine combination for a large pot: *Fuchsia* '**Annabel**' above white marguerites, helichrysum and variegated foliage.

4. HARDY FUCHSIAS

A number of fuchsias are frost-hardy and can be planted permanently outside in the garden in those areas where the winter permits this.

A Star of Late Summer

FLOWERS OF HARDY FUCHSIAS are produced in the late summer until frost damages them in the autumn or early winter. In mild regions the top growth will survive on the shrub throughout the winter; whereas it will fail during a prolonged spell of low temperatures. In this case, the plants die down to ground level during winter. In spring, cut off the dead top growth. The fuchsias will produce new shoots from below the ground later in the spring.

'Eleanor Rawlins' A bushy, upright variety producing masses of medium-sized single blooms. The sepals are carmine with a magenta corolla, carmine at the base.

'Margaret' is a vigorous shrub. Here, beside a wall it reaches up to 1.5m/5ft within a single season. The colours of the flowers are enriched by bronze fennel.

Hardy fuchsias can be successfully planted to adorn paved areas where their blooms can be viewed from all angles.

Hardy fuchsias can be incorporated in herbaceous borders, as (in frosty areas) they die down to ground level during the winter and grow harmoniously beside their neighbours in the spring. In this group, the intense red and purple flowers of '**Mrs Popple**' co-ordinate well with the blue *Aconitum carmichaelii* and the leaves of the **purple sage**, and provide a rich deep background to the **lavender 'Hidcote'** in front.

HARDY FUCHSIAS

F. magellanica gracilis 'Variegata' Long arching stems are clothed with variegated cream, green and pink leaves.

◆ *The coloured foliage gives an additional attraction to this variety.*

F. magellanica 'Alba' This variety sports bright green foliage bearing small single flowers with pale lilac sepals and deeper lilac corolla.

The golden foliage of **F. magellanica 'Aurea'** provides a beautiful contrast to the green leaves and red-purple flowers of **'Bambini'**.

'Army Nurse' Vigorous, upright-growing variety. Small deep rose-pink sepals, purple corolla, veined with pink.

'Pee Wee Rose' This small single red-flowered fuchsia contrasts delightfully with the mass of finely cut silver leaves of artemisia.

F. magellanica 'Aurea' forms an impressive background to the dwarf-growing **'Tom Thumb'**.

'Dollar Princess' Sturdy, bushy, free-branching variety yielding quantities of medium-sized, double flowers. Cerise sepals with a purple corolla.

◆ *Tends to flower slightly later than most varieties.*

'Lena' produces an arching bush, bearing medium-sized double blooms. Pale pink sepals, deep pink corolla.

◆ Clematis *'Jackmanii Superba'* intertwined with the fuchsia adds interest to the plant.

'Margaret Brown' Profuse-flowering, upright bush, sporting small single blooms. Rose-pink sepals, with a pale rose corolla.

'Checkerboard' Vigorous, upright-growing single with thin white curved sepals below a red tube and deep red corolla.

'Whiteknights Blush' The dark green leaves of this hardy fuchsia show off the delicate blush-pink blooms to perfection.

'Genii' Upright, bushy habit with yellow-green foliage and red stems. Small, single flowers of cerise and purple.

Bedding Plants

Bedding plants are invaluable in the garden as they provide a continuous carpet of colour for a long period during spring and summer. They can be grown to great effect in borders next to the house, also beside lawns and paths. Island beds of various shapes and sizes can be introduced to enhance lawns, paved and gravelled areas. Essentially the beds should be formal in nature, providing a co-ordinated display.

During recent years many gardeners have resorted to planting perennials in their borders to reduce expense and labour. Shrubs and herbaceous plants, although a good compromise, don't provide such a lasting wealth of colour and adornment. They also command sizeable areas of ground when mature, which is acceptable in large gardens but unsatisfactory in small ones. Consequently, if you would like a dazzling display to beautify your house and garden, there is no substitute for the planting of annual bedding plants.

PLANNING YOUR BEDDING SCHEME
The range of plants and cultivars at your disposal is vast, especially in the case of summer

Narcissi and double daisies on a grand scale.

49

Cascading pelargoniums for baskets or window boxes.

Echium 'Blue Bedder' is a reliable hardy annual.

bedding. Many factors have to be considered when designing your proposed scheme.

1. Aspect, size and shape of borders.
2. Predominance of sunshine or shade.
3. Preferred colour pattern.
4. Relative heights of adjacent plants on maturity.
5. Planting distances. These will determine the number of plants required.
6. Cost of acquiring plants. This may influence the types chosen and the method of production.
7. Availability of the beds, if already occupied by your previous display.

This planning exercise is always pleasurable, especially if it is embarked upon during winter evenings by the fire. Seed catalogues, with their glossy images, are designed to seduce the enterprising gardener. They almost always succeed in persuading you to try new, ever more alluring varieties, which provide key points of interest in the forthcoming display.

ACQUIRING YOUR PLANTS

Once you have designed your bedding scheme, a decision has to be made as to how the plants are to be obtained. Traditionally, most bedding plants were raised by the gardener from seed in a greenhouse. This approach was the most rewarding, but required time and dedication.

Nowadays, several other options are available. Many seed firms and garden centres supply packs of seedlings ready for 'pricking out' (planting) into containers. Larger plants in the form of 'plugs' growing in individual cells, can also be grown on. Otherwise, garden centres and nurseries provide an extensive variety of mature plants ready for bedding-out into the border. This course is to be advocated where time and production facilities are absent.

GROWING FROM SEED

It is always exciting in the early spring to sow the first of your bedding plants in the greenhouse. The sowing times and cultural information about each variety are always documented on the seed packets. At this stage it is important to sow sufficient seed to produce the requisite number of plants for your scheme.

Many seeds, such as impatiens (busy lizzies), begonias, salvias etc., need warm seed compost in which to germinate. This can be provided by using a propagator which contains an electrically heated base, on which the pots or trays are placed. Alternatively, the germination process can be omitted by purchasing young plants of difficult subjects.

The sowing of small seeds is helped by mixing them with dry fine sand; this mix can then be sprinkled evenly over the level surface of the compost. Generally, seeds need only a light covering of fine sand or compost. Glass and newspaper are then placed over the container to keep the seeds warm and in the dark until the seedlings start to emerge.

Once the seedlings are large enough to handle and before they become spindly due to overcrowding, they are pricked out into bedding-plant compost in the greenhouse. Seed trays serve as the customary container

Tulips and double daisies give a dazzling display.

but an array of various sized 'cell trays' and pots are also available in which to grow plants with their own separate root systems. These remain in the greenhouse until they have utilized the space afforded them. They should then be large enough to transfer to the borders.

'Hardening off' the young plants acclimatizes them to outdoor conditions prior to planting. A cold frame is ideal for this purpose, as you can control temperature and watering according to the prevailing weather conditions. In the case of summer bedding plants, night frosts in spring present the greatest hazard and plants must be suitably protected.

PREPARATION OF THE BORDER

Prior to planting, the soil requires forking and breaking down to a fine tilth. A balanced fertilizer should be incorporated and the ground raked smooth. When planting large beds, it is advisable to mark them out with lines to determine the position of the plants. Sand or lime sprinkled over the prepared bed facilitates this. Several criteria affect the decision on when to plant your beds.

1. Resident plants of a previous bedding scheme may still be attractive.
2. The state of maturity of your young plants – are they strong enough?
3. Can night frosts be disregarded?
4. The border soil may be too wet or too dry.
5. You need to find the time and motivation to begin the job.

To maintain your border you must, first and foremost, guard against slug damage. In the country, however, rabbits or other pests may prove to be an even greater problem when they arrive for their breakfast. Watering is necessary during dry periods, especially until the plants become established. Weeds will also need to be removed.

Your bedding plants should now reward your efforts and produce an ever more spectacular riot of colour.

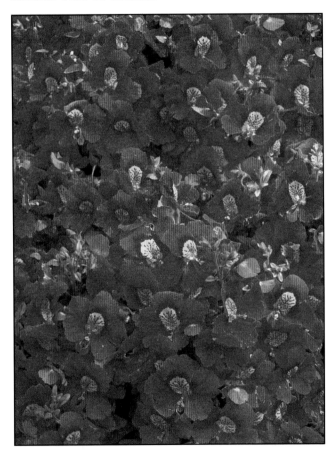

(*Above*) *Schizanthus* 'Hit Parade' or poor man's orchid.

(*Right*) Double daisies (*Bellis* 'Medici Rose') surround *Ornithogalum nutans*.

1. SPRING BEDDING

Bedding plants that flower in spring must be planted in the autumn, so need to withstand the frosts and wet of winter.

The myriads of flowers of the **myosotis** (forget-me-not) create an immaculate foil for the exquisite lily-flowered **tulip 'China Pink'**. The stems and leaves rise gracefully above the blue haze to parade the soft pink hues of the overlapping reflexed petals.

DURING PROLONGED COLD PERIODS, bedding plants become frozen and stop flowering. However, as spring approaches, they gradually come to life and reward us with ever increasing colourful displays of flowers. This transforms our garden into a cheerful and inviting oasis.

Polyanthus require rich, moist, well drained soil in which to excel. Plant 30cm/1ft apart during early autumn.

◆ *The tulips follow an earlier display of daffodils.*

Universal pansies are planted 25cm/10in apart during autumn or spring.

◆ *Planting of summer bedding is often delayed as the pansies are in their prime.*

The contrasting drifts of **wallflowers, daisies** and **tulips** create a beautiful kaleidoscope of colour.

◆ *The terraces enhance the display by raising the plants.*

Displays *for* Spring

FLOWERS ARE AT A PREMIUM during winter and early spring. Formerly, wallflowers and myosotis (forget-me-nots) were the traditional spring bedding plants, but the introduction of winter-flowering pansies has transformed the spring garden with an extensive colour range and long flowering-period. Ample reward is afforded for your efforts as you watch the first precocious blooms braving the elements.

Wallflowers and **Tulips**
Single contrasting colours produce a more uniform display as all the plants grow and flower evenly, unlike mixed varieties. The tulips must always grow taller than their host plant so that their blooms are visible.

Wallflowers Well-branched plants should be planted 37cm/15in apart during early autumn. They thrive in well drained sunny borders and dislike waterlogged conditions. Fragrant. 30 × 30cm/1 × 1ft

DISPLAYS *for* SPRING

'Ultima' and 'Universal' pansies will flower during mild periods in winter and continue into the summer. 15 × 23cm/6 × 9in

The pansies provide a background of continuous colour, whilst the narcissi gradually emerge and dominate the display.

◆ *The pansies will reassert themselves once the narcissi have flowered.*

Bellis perennis (**Double daisies**) are available in shades of white, red and pink. They are ideal as an edging plant or for mass displays, interplanted with tulips. 15 × 23cm/6 × 9in

Daisies, polyanthus and wallflowers harmonize beautifully. The tulips provide the icing on the cake, decorating the wallflowers.

◆ *This demonstrates that mixed varieties can be integrated alongside self-coloured types.*

Myosotis (Forget-me-not) makes the ideal edging plant, or as a mass interplanted with tulips. 15 × 30cm/6in × 1ft

CULTURAL NOTES

It is important to bed out your scheme during early autumn so that the plants become established before winter. Growth ceases during frosty weather.

Once the bedding plants are in position, bulbs can be inserted in the gaps between them.

Little maintenance is required after planting, as normally sufficient rain falls from the heavens and weed growth is thankfully minimal.

This is a colourful combination but the tulips can become lost amongst the polyanthus due to insufficient contrast.

Primroses grown in pots in the greenhouse and planted out in early spring produce a dazzling display. Fragrant. 10 × 15cm/4 × 6in

◆ *They are the 'Rolls Royce' of bedding. However, cost may prove prohibitive.*

SPRING BULBS

Hyacinths produce tubular spikes of florets which give off an exceptionally heavy fragrance, providing an extra aura in your garden.

Hyacinths can be planted out in the garden after being forced for use in the house.

Daffodils turn their flowers towards the sun. Remember to plant them in a position where they will face you too.

Except in a very formal scheme, avoid bedding out plants in rows. They will look more comfortable if intermingled.

Tulips like sun and a summer baking. In cold wet regions they are best lifted and stored in the dry before being replanted.

'L'Innocence' is an established hyacinth producing large sturdy spikes of beautiful white bells. 20cm/8in

***Narcissus* 'Sir Winston Churchill'** Vigorous, scented daffodil suitable for interplanting with wallflowers. 37cm/1ft 3in

***Narcissus* 'Roseworthy'** Delicate white petals of the perianth encircle the fluted salmon trumpet. 30cm/1ft

***Narcissus* 'Thalia'** produces up to three pure white blooms per stem. Ideal for the front edge of a border. 30cm/1ft

***Narcissus* 'Jenny'** Free-flowering, cyclamineus type. Suitable for fronts of borders and containers. 25cm/10in

Crocus Invaluable for providing colour in early spring. Broadcast bulbs in grass in the autumn and plant 5cm/2in deep.

◆ *Delay mowing in the spring until leaves have turned brown.*

Muscari (Grape hyacinth) Very easily grown in all types of soil and situations. Useful for edging and colour in difficult locations.

BULBS PROVIDE EXTRA COLOUR and add interest to your spring display. Many, moreover, unlike bedding plants, are perennial and invariably multiply over the years, giving excellent value for money. Many hybrid tulips are the exception to this rule but they are worth treating as bedding plants.

Tulipa **'Noranda'** belongs to a late-flowering group of beautiful tulips whose petals have a crystal-like fringe. 45cm/1½ft

◆ *Pansies form the pale carpet beneath the tulips.*

Tulipa kaufmanniana **'Gaiety'** Commonly called the 'Waterlily Tulip'. This type is dwarf and very early flowering. 15cm/6in

◆ *The flowers require sunlight to open so plant in a south-facing situation.*

Allium aflatunense **'Purple Sensation'**, rises above pink forget-me-nots and white lychnis. 1m/3ft

◆ *This is a stunning, original mix of perennials and bedding for late spring.*

2. SUMMER BEDDING

Summer presents the gardener with a huge variety of plants for both formal and informal schemes.

PLANNING *the* SCHEME

YOU CAN PAINT A COLOURFUL DESIGN in your garden by using formal bedding schemes throughout the summer months. Conversely, informal displays, though often lacking visual impact, provide a continuity of interest as they evolve. The taller kinds of tobacco flower (nicotiana) are especially graceful in such arrangements.

Triphylla fuchsias create dark rich islands of colour amongst a drift of the marguerite, **Argyranthemum 'Jamaica Primrose'**.

◆ *The contrasts of height and colour create an effective display.*

Impatiens, nicotiana and **ageratum** arranged in linear composition on a tiered border.

◆ *Respective heights of plants must be taken into consideration.*

A small-scale formal bedding display of mixed annuals in a domestic setting.

◆ *The grey-leaved cineraria makes a striking 'dot plant'.*

64

The realm of summer bedding
embraces a wealth of plant forms,
from the tall growing *Nicotiana*
'Sensation' with its single star-shaped
blooms and the large double flowers
of **zinnia**, to the dwarf **alyssum**
clothed with myriads of minute
florets.

TALLER PLANTS

When planting remember to allocate adequate space as they may eventually grow over and smother their neighbours.

Additional support in the form of canes or sticks may be required.

TALL PLANTS located at the back or at the centre of borders provide variety and height. The selection here embraces annuals to be sown straight into the ground, half-hardy plants, bulbs, tubers and frost-tender shrubs which can be housed under glass in cold areas and planted out in the summer.

Asters flower later in the summer and are useful for providing colour when some bedding plants are waning. ○

Argyranthemum **'Vancouver'** This free-flowering marguerite is a half-hardy perennial propagated from cuttings. ○

Clarkia and the dwarf **candytuft** give a harmonious display when sown on site. Although not 'bedded out' these annuals achieve striking effects in a season. ○

◆ *These are good as 'fillers' and for creating colour in a dull spot.*

Cleome hassleriana **'Colour Fountain'** forms an idyllic background for the free-flowering *Penstemon* 'Garnet'. ○

Helianthus, the sunflower, is a favourite with children for its extra large blooms and height (2.2m/7ft). ○

Lilium 'Mont Blanc' can be utilized where height is required, without the plant spreading over its neighbour.

Abutilons Half-hardy shrubs which can be grown outside during summer and in a frost-free greenhouse in winter.

Helichrysum (Strawflower) provide a dazzling show of colour and are a favourite annual for dried flower arrangements. ○

Cosmos is a vigorous, bushy, upright annual and a most graceful addition to a scheme. Moist, well-drained soil. ○

Clockwise from top-left: a medium decorative dahlia; a cactus dahlia; a pompon dahlia; *Dahlia* 'Moonfire'.

◆ *Each of these types grows to about 1m/3ft and the tubers need to be planted at this distance. Half-hardy.* ○

PLANTS *of* MEDIUM HEIGHT

The hardy annual **Centaurea cyanus** (Cornflower) grows easily in any type of soil but requires plenty of light. ○

The flowers of **Salpiglossis 'Casino'**, a purple bicolour, can be used as cut flowers, although they are sticky to handle. ○

Dianthus barbatus (Sweet William) has a short flowering period and is usually grown as a hardy biennial. ○

The unusual colour of the mallow, **Malva sylvestris 'Primley Blue'**, is not readily found in other summer bedding subjects. ○

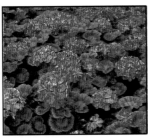

Zonal pelargoniums (Geraniums) are amongst the elite of bedding plants. They produce vivid displays during dry summers. ○

The dark red **nicotiana** form a good background for the pale pink **pelargoniums** edged with mauve **ageratum**.

◆ *This illustrates a perfect graduation of plants of differing heights.*

Heliotrope produces dark green, deep veined leaves which support corymbs of fragrant forget-me-not-like flowers. ○

Salmon **pelargoniums** are interspersed with mauve **verbena** and an edging is provided by alternating lemon-yellow **marigolds** with mauve **ageratum**.

◆ *This shows how to co-ordinate colours in an arrangement using different subjects.*

INFORMAL BEDDING SCHEMES are becoming more commonplace. Plants flowering throughout the summer can be incorporated into an existing bed or border to create extra colour. Many of the tender perennials, like the salvia below which can be grown early in the year from seed, are charming in informal schemes.

Nicotiana produce a profusion of blooms throughout the summer, and emit a sweet perfume during the evening.

Salvia patens produces vivid blue flowers and is useful as a 'filler' in informal bedding schemes of blue and yellow.

All of these plants illustrated require sunny aspects to perform well.

Plants which flower over the longest possible period should be chosen for formal bedding.

Salmon **nicotiana** overlook the brighter coral carpet of **impatiens**. Both of these plants produce spectacularly colourful displays over an exceptionally long period.

◆ *They thrive on warmth, therefore do not plant out too early.*

69

PLANTS *of* MEDIUM HEIGHT

White *Osteospermum* 'Whirligig' growing amongst blue nemophila requires a sunny situation for its flowers to open. ○

Sweet pea 'Snoopea' is unique in that it has no tendrils. The plant channels all its energy into producing flowers. ○

Tagetes produce masses of small orange flowers throughout the summer and the foliage emits a pungent smell if bruised. ○

Lantana are grown from seeds or cuttings and produce flowers throughout the summer months. ○

A formal bed of mixed coloured **African marigolds** with an araucaria (monkey puzzle) as a centre piece. ○

The uniformity of shape of these **African marigolds** is relieved by the mix of lemons and oranges. ○

Antirrhinums are among the first bedding plants able to be planted out and may survive another year in mild winters. ○

Large flowering *Tagetes erecta* (African marigold) produces vigorous, erect, well-branched plants, requiring space. ○

THE BRILLIANCE of many summer bedding plants can be utilized to produce large areas of colour in formal beds or to improve any dull or uninteresting part of the garden. Each year there is something new in the seed catalogues or garden centres to tantalize us. So be adventurous with your bedding scheme and you will always arouse interest and provide the element of surprise.

Purple **verbena** harmonizes with dark red **salvia**. The lemon **marigolds** and silver **cineraria** provide a lighter contrast. ○

The mixed informal planting of summer bedding subjects succeeds in adorning a stone wall.

Tagetes patula (French marigold) are available in shades of yellow and bronze, as well as bicolours. ○

During prolonged dry spells, watering is essential to maintain the production of flowers.

Marigolds are prone to damage by slugs when planted out. Protective measures must be taken.

71

DWARF PLANTS

Dwarf plants will provide a carpet of colour in which to position standard fuchsias as focal points.

The bright golden, daisy-shaped flowers of *Gazania* **'Dorothy'**, require a light sunny position to remain open.

Felicia amelloides (**Blue marguerite**) produces masses of small blue star-shaped Michaelmas daisy type blooms all summer. ○

The charming lilac *Nemesia fruticans* will flower all summer if dead-headed. Will tolerate light shade.

This carefully worked out bedding scheme has been arranged to flow gracefully around the existing evergreens: a conifer and hebe.

Chrysanthemum parthenium has pungently aromatic light green leaves with hosts of long-lasting flowers. ○

Verbena produce bright, rich coloured clusters of primrose-like fragrant flowers over a long period. ○

Salvia splendens is a classical formal bedding plant, producing a blaze of scarlet blooms on uniform compact plants. ○

◆ *Very tender plants which must not be planted out too early.*

Linaria maroccana '**Fairy Bouquet**' is available in distinct shades of pinks and mauves. ○

Schizanthus '**Hit Parade**', the poor man's orchid, produces a wealth of blooms above deeply divided fern-like foliage. ○

Sweet pea 'Cupid Mixed' gives an abundance of scented flowers on a dwarf, bushy plant, which does not need staking. ○

Many of the plants illustrated here may be used as edging plants in the front of borders.

A dwarf **pelargonium** of the Angel group. Easily raised from cuttings, it has bushy growth and flowers that resemble violas. ○

Stocks can be grown in virtually any soil in a sunny position. They have a short flowering period but are very scented.

Begonia × *tuberhybrida* are among the elite of bedding plants and require fertile, sheltered conditions, with plenty of moisture, in order to excel.

◆ *The silver foliage of cineraria enhances the display with its contrasting colour.*

EDGING PLANTS

When planting beside a lawn, leave enough space to allow you to edge the grass as the plants mature.

***Senecio maritima* 'Silver Dust'** (cineraria) is used essentially for its attractive, white felted, fern-like foliage. ○

Begonia semperflorens are extremely free-flowering and are able to survive a hot sunny dry position.

Echeverias are advantageous for hot dry spots as their rosettes of leathery leaves resist drought. ○

Impatiens (Busy Lizzie) are grown extensively as they can be relied on to produce carpets of colour in the garden, from planting until the autumn frosts.

◆ *They must be watered regularly during dry interludes if they are to thrive.*

Calendula (marigold) is one of the oldest of bedding plants. It thrives in the poorest of soils and readily self-seeds. ○

Lobularia maritima (*Alyssum maritimum*) is a traditional edging plant and is available in shades of white, pink and lilac. ○

FORMAL FLOWER BEDS are traditionally edged with compact, dwarf plants. Single colours or varieties may be used, or several can be alternated, to create contrasting effects. A thin line of plants forming a ribbon will always look formal or artificial; flowing drifts of varying width will seem more relaxed especially if the plants are chosen to spill forward.

Petunia **'Ultra Star'** series give excellent displays during dry periods but flowers turn brown in prolonged wet weather. ○

Colour co-ordinate your edge with the other plants in the border so that they produce a suitable contrast.

Diascias are some of the most prolific flowering plants. They thrive in a sunny situation but require watering to perform well.

Mesembryanthemum (Livingstone daisy) thrives in dry sunny sites as the brilliant flowers only open in bright sunshine.

Osteospermums continually produce white or mauve daisy-shaped blooms which close up towards evening.

Iberis (candytuft) is a free-flowering plant which will tolerate poor soil conditions and a dry situation. ○

Ageratum produces compact mounds of flowers over a long period. ○

◆ *Another good blue half-hardy annual is lobelia.*

'DOT' PLANTS

Senecio maritimus (Cineraria) can be planted to form islands of silver foliage rising above carpets of **impatiens**.

The broad upright majestic leaves and bright flowers of the **canna** dominate the brilliant poppy-like flowers of **eschscholzia** bordered with the silver perennial *Stachys byzantina* (Lamb's ears).

'DOT' PLANTS

The large palmate leaves of ***Ricinus communis*** (Castor oil plant) make an unusual and interesting focal point amid drifts of **impatiens**.

'DOT' PLANTS PROVIDE FOCAL POINTS of interest among areas of summer bedding. They can be short or tall, and they can form an isolated incident, or be inserted to form a repeat planting at intervals, but in either case it is essential that they must distinguish themselves from their surrounding bedding. Usually large pot-grown subjects are bought or raised at home under glass for this purpose, and then put in the ground at a suitable time for planting.

Angel's Trumpet (Brugmansia, syn. datura) Impressive focal point if grown as a standard. ○

◆ *Grow amongst heliotrope for a wonderfully scented combination.*

77

The Flower Garden

EVERYONE LOVES A FLOWER GARDEN. For it is here that a multitude of delightful and lovely plants can be brought together into a picturesque whole. The combining of colour, the consideration of form and the appreciation of texture will all contribute to harmonious and pleasing flower borders.

Shaping the Borders

Traditionally borders mark the edge of a lawn, follow the line of a path or front an adjacent feature such as a wall, hedge or fence. Today the name also applies to free-standing or island beds as well as those which encompass sweeps and curves.

For a formal effect, symmetrically shaped borders of squares, rectangles and circles are best. Thought should be given to proportion and, ideally, one border will be matched by another of equal size and shape.

This is very confident use of colour whereby brilliant effects have been achieved through combining hues at the hot end of the scale – gold, burnt orange and ruby – toned down by the sombre purple-brown of foliage. The shapes of the group are also interesting. The flat flower heads of the achillea at the rear contrast with the sword leaves of the crocosmia.

In cool, moist part-shade, *Primula florindae* (Giant cowslip) rises above orange mimulus.

POSITIONING PLANTS

Border preparation is essential if flowering plants are to perform well. Following the removal of all perennial weeds and coarse grasses, the ground should be well dug to incorporate plenty of organic matter. Heavy or poorly drained soil may be improved by the addition of well rotted compost, sharp sand, bonfire ash or horticultural grit.

Container-grown plants allow planting at virtually any time although extremes of weather should be avoided. It is worth taking trouble when planting to give plants the best possible start. For this a good-sized hole needs to be dug to which should be added mature compost. Once removed from their pots, plants should be placed to a depth which corresponds with the original soil mark. Where a strong root system exists, roots may be gently teased out before filling in the hole and firming round to eliminate any air pockets. A thorough watering should then be given.

The way in which a border faces, the aspect, and the amount of sun or shade it receives has a bearing on what will grow. An open, sunny site with some shelter at the rear is ideal for many sun-loving plants. Shade, cast by a canopy of tree leaves, from which there may well be 'drip', prevents certain plants from flourishing.

The degree of alkalinity or acidity of the soil, measured on a pH scale, determines what will thrive. A pH of 7.0 indicates a neutral soil, above is alkaline, below acid. Some plants will not tolerate lime and will only succeed on acid soils with a low pH. Others demand more alkaline conditions.

Borders made up of generous curves, with an absence of straight lines, can give an illusion of space. Island beds create a softening impression and serve to break the monotony of a large area.

Personal preference, taste and the requirements of the site will all determine layout. Certainly the final arrangement will take into account the need to show plants to their best possible advantage.

Wallflowers in mingled shades of buttery yellow and dark red are a scented addition to a patio.

The spotted leopard lily (*Lilium pardalinum*) produces its turkscap flowers in summer.

Lilium 'King Pete', a robust low-growing lily, also flowers in summer. It will do well in a large pot which can be placed on a terrace or even positioned in a bed.

THEMES AND SCHEMES

Winter lends itself to the job of border planning when the days are short and outside activities are curtailed. Plant catalogues and seed lists are excellent sources to be pored over and from which selections may be made. By drawing out the flower border to scale, and plotting the position of plants, a pleasing and successful display is guaranteed.

Colour planning is a matter of personal choice. In a small garden a mixed-colour border may be preferred where plants are chosen as much for height and spread and flowering period as for colour. A blaze of brightly coloured plants may well appeal with strong reds placed alongside brilliant yellows. Alternatively the combination of pastel shades creates a subtle, tranquil effect. Where space permits, single-colour borders can give an air of sophistication. However, no scheme should be adhered to too rigidly for very often the introduction of another single colour serves to highlight and intensify the principal colour. The flowers of a blue border are made more special when set against a foil of silver and grey leaves. A yellow arrangement of lemons through to deep gold, complemented by variegated foliage, is a bright scheme for a dreary day. The introduction of white, or mid blue, enhances the design.

If room allows, blocks of plants of a single variety placed together make an immediate

The classic well-loved combination of the tulip 'China Pink' and forget-me-nots.

THE FLOWERS

Mixing together annuals, biennials, perennials and bulbs in the flower borders will give colour and interest for the greater part of the year.

A hardy annual completes its life cycle in one year. Grown from seed it will germinate, flower, set seed and die within a single season. Seeds are usually sown in the open ground in the spring. Half-hardy annuals behave in exactly the same manner but the seed needs to be sown under cover. Young plants are set out when the threat of frosts is past.

In contrast a biennial requires two seasons. During the first it will produce stems and leaves, delaying flowering until the second when it too will set seed and die.

Perennial plants will establish and remain in the border for a number of years. As a general rule they make new growth in the spring, flower, then die down in the winter. Not all are totally hardy and some may not survive severe weather conditions. Others are evergreen and so do not completely disappear.

Bulbs and corms and tubers consist of fleshy organs which, when planted, will grow for many seasons.

impact. Planted in groups of threes, fives, sevens or more, such an arrangement ensures flowers, and therefore interest, over a long period. As an alternative, set clumps of the same plant to flower in informal drifts. The repetition of a particular flower, a spot plant, adds unity to the scheme and carries the eye forward.

PLANT CARE

Weeding the borders in the early part of the year results in much labour saved later on. Where possible the application of a mulch, some form of organic matter, to a depth of about 7.5cm/3in promotes healthy and vigorous plants. Additionally, a mulch reduces water evaporation during dry periods. As flowers develop, a liquid feed may be applied.

(*Above*) *Penstemon* 'Edithiae' is low-growing, bushy and in flower from spring to early summer. Although unfussy about soil conditions, it prefers full sun. Stocks can be readily increased by taking cuttings in the later part of the year.

The shrub *Lavatera* 'Burgundy Wine' is visible through an airy haze of *Verbena bonariensis* which is a marvellous plant for the front of a border as it adds interest and is see-through. It self-seeds gently and doesn't need staking.

For this purpose a wide range of fertilizers is available. Manufacturers' instructions should be followed exactly.

As plants begin to grow, those of less robust habit will need some form of staking to protect them from wind and rain. For lower-growing, smaller plants it is sufficient to drive in three or four sticks around the plant and tie these with string. Hazel or birch twigs are ideal for this. Taller, stronger-growing specimens require a more substantial approach of bamboo canes or manufactured stakes. These should be put in place early in the season; further staking and tying may be necessary at intervals.

Unfortunately, periodically flowers are attacked by pests, virus or fungal disease. The nature and intensity of any attack will vary from season to season. Where diseases are detected at an early stage and treatment carried out, control is relatively easy. In many instances, particularly in the case of pests, Nature herself will take charge. It must be remembered that not all insects are harmful in the garden. Many are not only harmless but helpful.

1. EARLY SPRING

Thoughts of winter are set aside as the first buds burst. Fragile flowers announce the start of a new season.

FIRST FLOWERS

PERHAPS NOTHING IS MORE WELCOME in the garden than the first sightings of spring flowers to mark the end of the drab days of winter.

A small jug of blooms from the early spring garden dominated by the delicate violet petals of *Iris unguicularis* (Algerian iris).

PLANNING AHEAD

Now is the time to order seeds of annuals for summer displays.

Sow half-hardy annuals under glass to plant out when the threat of frost is past.

Hardy annuals may be sown directly into well prepared seed-beds where they are to bloom.

Winter-flowering heathers provide bold clumps of glowing colour throughout early spring. They thrive in well drained soil.

◆ *Heathers should be clipped hard back as the flowers die. Fresh foliage will soon emerge.*

Galanthus '**Magnet**' This snowdrop's tiny flowers stand proud above grey-green sword-like leaves to brave the worst of weather. ◑, ● 10cm/4in

Cyclamen coum is available in many different forms. Leaves are often interestingly marbled. ◑, 10cm/4in

◆ *Cyclamen are ideal subjects for dry situations where little else will grow.*

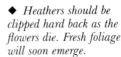

Snowdrops are ideally grown in a woodland situation
although they will prosper in cool, moist soil at the base
of a sunless wall. Here they look splendid in contrast to
the deep red leaves of bergenia.

◆ *Division of snowdrops should take place after
flowering but before the foliage has died down.*

FIRST FLOWERS

EARLY SPRING BULBS come into their own at this time of year to provide warmth and cheer to the borders. Most are suited to growing under deciduous trees and shrubs where, later in the year, their dying foliage will be concealed. With careful planning it is possible to have a succession of bulbs in flower.

Anemone blanda is a plant for the edge of woodland. Its many petalled blooms are usually of mid-blue. 10 cm/4in

Chionodoxa luciliae The common name, Glory of the Snow, well describes these pretty bluish-lilac flowers. 10cm/4in

Crocus are amongst the most versatile of bulbs. Grow in the border or in pots, in sun or in shade.

◆ *Mature bulbs should be planted about 5cm/2in deep and 10cm/4in apart.*

Crocus tommasinianus should be placed in drifts in an open position and left undisturbed to naturalize. 10cm/4in

Primula denticulata The drumstick primula is happiest in moisture-retentive soil. ◗, 20 × 30cm/8in × 1ft

Narcissus bulbocodium
Long trumpets of clear yellow distinguish this early flowering, small daffodil.
○, 15–20cm/6–8in

Narcissus cyclamineus is particularly distinctive with its protruding trumpet and reflexed perianth segments.
15–20cm/6–8in

Narcissus 'February Gold'
This miniature daffodil enjoys damp soil and is an excellent choice for rough grass. 15–20cm/6–8in

POT PLANTS

Many of the small spring bulbs are ideally suited to be grown in pots or as additions to sink gardens. Ensure plenty of drainage by placing several crocks at the bottom of the pot. Plant in suitable growing compost to which has been added a good measure of horticultural grit. A light dressing of a low nitrogen fertilizer in autumn and early spring will ensure healthy growth.

Narcissus 'Tête-à-Tête' A robust little hybrid which produces more than one flower on each stem. Provided with good drainage, it makes a worthwhile choice for a terracotta pot.
15–20cm/6–8in

Iris reticulata 'Harmony'
This blue iris is an early flowering dwarf form for a sunny position.
10–15cm/4–6in

◆ *Propagate the reticulata irises by lifting and dividing the bulbs in late summer.*

89

STARTING *in* STYLE

Iris unguicularis Place the Algerian iris in a pot to stand beside an entrance or doorway for its brief but lovely flowering period. E, ◑, 20 × 60cm/ 8in × 2ft

CULTIVATING HELLEBORES

Hellebores enjoy rich conditions. An annual mulch of well rotted compost or a liberal application of leaf mould will be beneficial.

As the flowers of *Helleborus orientalis* (Lenten rose) unfold, remove all the previous year's leaves. This makes for a tidier plant and shows off the flowers to good effect.

Euphorbia rigida Glaucous leaves make this a most striking spurge to be grown in a sunny position. ◑, E, 60 × 45cm/ 1 × 1½ft

◆ *Euphorbias are poisonous plants. Contact with skin may cause irritation.*

***Helleborus foetidus* 'Wester Flisk'** has greyish-green leaves with distinctive, red-tinged flower stalks. E, ◑, 45 × 45cm/1½ × 1½ft

NO SPRING BORDER should be without aristocratic hellebores, lovely early-flowering iris or the majestic spurge, *Euphorbia rigida*. In a period of the year when the weather is often discouraging, these flowers transform the garden, bringing to it both colour and interest.

It is not simply the range of hues from purest white to deepest black, but the limitless variations of shading, veining and spotting that make *Helleborus orientalis* such magical plants.

SHADE LOVERS

As SPRING UNFOLDS, the sun's rays reach down through the bare branches of trees to bosky clearings where life begins to stir. Before they are overshadowed by a canopy of leaves, early plants burst into flower.

Primula **'Dusky Lady'** Dark and mysterious, this deeply coloured primula has a long flowering season.
15 × 15cm/6 × 6in

Primula **'Hose-in-Hose'** Unusual for flowering above a tiny ruff of leaves.
10 × 10cm/4 × 4in

Epimedium × *youngianum* **'Roseum'** From a base of attractive leaves rise stems of tiny rose-coloured flowers.
25 × 30cm/10in × 1ft

Epimedium × *youngianum* **'Niveum'** Small white flowers are eye-catching in the early part of the year.
25 × 30cm/10in × 1ft

Omphalodes cappadocica **'Cherry Ingram'** Early on, this is a reluctant flowerer. Later it will be a mass of blue. 15 × 30cm/6in × 1ft

Hugging the floor of the woodland, the winter aconite vies with the snowdrop to be amongst the first flowers of spring. Its glossy, bright yellow buttercup flowers, overtopping a ruff of deeply cut leaves, will make a splash of gold year after year if left undisturbed. The little blue *Iris histroides*, 10cm/4in tall, blooms slightly later.

Leucojum vernum
Sometimes known as the spring snowflake. The bell-shaped flower of six petals is tipped green.
20 × 10cm/8 × 4in

SHADE LOVERS

Euphorbia amygdaloides var. robbiae Bracts rather than flowers characterize this spurge for dry conditions. 75 × 75 cm/2½ × 2½ft

Scilla mischtschenkoana (S. tubergeniana) Flowers of a fragile blue to enliven an otherwise dull corner. 10 × 7.5cm/4 × 3in

Vinca minor 'Burgundy' An exceptional coloured form of the spreading lesser periwinkle in bloom from mid-spring to autumn. 15 × 60cm+/6in × 2ft+

Anemone apennina The blue flowers of this pretty species become flattened stars in the spring sun. 10 × 7.5cm/4 × 3in

◆ *Grow erythroniums amongst apennine anemones for a sparkling carpet of bloom.*

Cardamine trifolia This delicate little lady's smock delights with tiny flowers of pink or white. 20 × 30cm/8in x 1ft

SHEETS OF WOOD ANEMONE in the wild are one of the delights of springtime. A little too vigorous for the small garden, they rapidly increase by creeping rhizomes to form large pools of white. Placed alongside some of the early flowering narcissus they work well under leafless shrubs.

Cardamine pratensis **'Flore Pleno'** A very pretty double flower which has been in cultivation for several centuries. 20 × 30cm/ 8in × 1ft

Anemone nemorosa **'Bowles' Purple'** is one of a number of cultivated forms of wood anemone. 15 × 30cm/6in × 1ft

◆ *Anemone nemorosa* 'Robinsoniana' *has lavender-blue flowers and may be more easily obtainable.*

2. SPRING

*All the promise of the gardening year
is encapsulated in the cheerful blooms
of spring.*

MASSED EFFECTS

DAFFODILS ANNOUNCE THE ARRIVAL OF SPRING. Whether in the wild or in the garden their assertive trumpets capture the imagination and bring cheer to the darkest of days.

Narcissus 'Ice Follies'
Opening pale lemon yellow, this daffodil gradually ages to white. 45cm/1½ft

Narcissus poeticus The pheasant's eye is beautifully scented.
◐, 45cm/1½ft

◆ *Remove dead heads after flowering but leave foliage to die down.*

Narcissus 'Hawera' Many bulbs are well suited to growing in gravel. Here 'Hawera' enjoys the good drainage. 45cm/1½ft

Muscari neglectum Dense spikes of blue typify the grape hyacinth which is tolerant of most situations. 10–15cm/4–6in

Brunnera macrophylla
(Siberian bugloss) Forget-me-not type flowers above good green foliage. ◑, 45 × 45cm/1½ × 1½ft

Aubrieta deltoidea A carpeter to spill over walls or paths. Cut back hard after flowering. ○, 5 × 45cm/2in × 1½ft

Myosotis No spring border should be without the much loved forget-me-not. Allow it to seed at will. 15 × 30cm/6in × 1ft

Saxifraga × urbium The common London pride should not be despised for it is the most serviceable of plants. 30 × 30cm/1 × 1ft

Alyssum saxatile will brighten the rock garden with its yellow flowers. ○, 15 × 30cm/6in × 1ft

Arabis caucasica A profusion of white flowers over evergreen foliage. Good for difficult spots. 15 × 30cm/6in × 1ft

MASSED EFFECTS

BULB CARE

For spring flowering, plant bulbs during the previous autumn.

As a broad guide bulbs should be planted to at least twice their depth.

Most bulbs may be allowed to remain in the ground although tulips and hyacinths may, if desired, be lifted once the leaves have died down.

An annual dressing of bonemeal lightly forked in before bulbs commence flowering will help to maintain vigour.

A white spring bed dominated by grouped planting of the impressive tulip 'Purissima' with white honesty and primroses.

◆ *Note the effect of repeat plantings of bold subjects.*

MASSED EFFECTS

BULBS FOR SHOW

Spring bulbs massed together are a joy to behold. For a stunning, continuous display, plant large quantities of one kind together. This avoids a spotted effect.

Choose bulbs with varying flower times. This will provide for a succession of colour over a long period.

Position bulbs amongst shrubs which will flower later to provide immediate interest and to extend the season.

Doronicum columnae Leopard's bane is an old-fashioned garden plant which continues to perform well. 45 × 45cm/1½ × 1½ft

Cheiranthus The heady fragrance of wallflowers is one of the many joys of spring. 30 × 30cm/1 × 1ft

◆ *Use wallflowers as early bedding (here with tulips) to be replaced later.*

Ranunculus Cultivated forms of celandine are well worth growing for their spring cheer. 10cm/4in

Phlox subulata This evergreen mound-former will gradually spread outwards to carpet the ground. ○, 20cm/8in

Polyanthus These cheerful spring flowers are a delight when planted closely in semi-shade. 15cm/6in

***Ajuga reptans* 'Catlin's Giant'** is a fine form of bugle with a metallic shine to the purple leaves. E, 15 × 60cm/6in × 2ft

TULIPS UNDERPLANTED WITH FORGET-ME-NOTS is a tried and tested marriage which never fails to please. The mix of bright colours captures the popular style of a cottage garden. Choosing a single variety of tulip, rather than different forms, will elevate the scheme to something rather special.

Here the new shoots of crocosmia provide a contrast of form and texture to the mass of forget-me-nots.

Tulipa **'China Pink'** A graceful lily-flowered tulip of pure satin pink with a white base. ○, 45cm/1½ft

Tulipa '**West Point**' Used in a planting with brunnera, the elegant, lemon-yellow flowers of the tulips contrast with the clear blue of the brunnera. ○, 45cm/1½ft

◆ *A good form of brunnera is 'Langtrees' with silver spotting on the leaves.*

SOMETHING UNUSUAL

THE CHOICE OF PLANTS AVAILABLE for the spring borders is limitless and no-one would be without many of the garden-worthy stalwarts which provide such promise at this time of year. The inclusion of something a little different adds certain style and transforms the conventional into the dramatic.

MAINTAINING APPEARANCES

Warmer days and the season's rain showers will produce many weed seedlings. Removing them now will be time well spent. In closely planted areas use a handfork. In more open ground a hoe will make light work of this task.

Dead-head spent flowers to prolong the flowering period and to keep plants looking good.

In dry periods water young plants to help them establish. Avoid surface watering. Water should be sufficient to penetrate the root system.

Uvularia grandiflora The bellwort prefers moist peaty soil. A most graceful spring plant. ☽, 30 × 30cm/1 × 1ft

Mertensia virginica A most appealing plant which is seldom seen. By mid-summer it has died down completely. ☽, 60 × 45cm/ 2 × 1½ft

Ipheion uniflorum 'Wisley Blue' Starry blue flowers are an enchanting addition to the front of the border. 15cm/6in

Erythronium dens-canis is but one of many dog's tooth violets enjoying a semi-shaded, humus rich situation. 15cm/6in

Pulmonaria 'Bowles' Blue' A beautiful lungwort and one of many available forms. ◐, 30 × 45cm/1 × 1½ft

Dicentra 'Bacchanal' is an exceptionally deep red bleeding heart with finely cut, glaucous green leaves. 30 × 30cm/1 × 1ft

Lysichiton americanus Yellow spathes and broad leaves are a feature of the moisture-loving skunk cabbage. 60 × 75cm/2 × 2½ft

Sanguinaria canadensis 'Plena' Unhappily the flowers of this marvellous little plant do not last for long. ◐, 10cm/4in

Camassia leichtlinii requires plenty of moisture when in growth. Effective near water or in grass. 75 × 30cm/2½ × 1ft

Darmera peltata (Umbrella plant) flowers from creeping rhizomes before the glossy leaves appear. 1m × 60cm/3 × 2ft

Fritillaria imperialis The crown imperial is one of the most majestic of garden plants and well worth growing. ○, 1m × 30cm/3 × 1ft

WOODLANDS ARE THE NATURAL HOME for many of our best loved spring plants. The early primroses, wood anemones and wild daffodils, later followed with sheets of bluebells, capture the very essence of the season. Not surprisingly many of these plants have been brought into garden cultivation. Even in a limited space it is possible to create the right growing environment in a garden setting for these woodlanders.

Primula veris To thrive the cowslip should be grown in grass in an open situation where it can benefit from full sun. Yellow flowers are often tinged orange or red. 20cm/8in

◆ *Less common in cultivation is the oxlip,* Primula elatior.

In the WILD

Pulsatilla vulgaris Several colour forms of the pasque flower are in cultivation. All require good drainage. 30 × 30cm/1 × 1ft

Viola odorata The leaves often tend to overpower the wonderfully scented, dainty flowers of the sweet violet. 10 × 30cm/4in × 1ft

Primula 'Valley Red' Primulas are an attractive addition to the less formal parts of the garden. ◑, 30 × 30cm/1 × 1ft

Scilla non-scripta Bluebells should mainly be reserved for the wild garden where, left undisturbed, they will naturalize. ◑, 25cm/10in

Caltha palustris A good choice for a damp spot beside a pond or stream. ◑, 60 × 60cm/2 × 2ft

Cardamine pratensis The lady's smock is to be found growing in damp meadows and ditches in the wild. ◑, 25cm/10in

Galium odoratum The sweet woodruff is a pleasing little carpeter with tiny, white star flowers for light shade. 20 × 30cm/8in × 1ft

BLUEBELLS AND POPPIES

For a really dashing scheme, plant bluebells with the yellow, and sometimes orange, Welsh poppy, *Meconopsis cambrica*. Both will increase readily from self-sown seed.

Primula vulgaris A cool shady bank makes an ideal site in which to place clumps of primroses. 10cm/4in

Meconopsis cambrica Allowed to seed around, the Welsh poppy will lend a casual air to the garden. 30 × 30cm/1 × 1ft

Convallaria majalis Beautifully scented, lily-of-the-valley will gradually increase over the years. ◑, ●, 20cm/8in

FLOWERING ALPINE MEADOWS are a source of inspiration. The impression of wild flowers sprinkled amongst gently waving grasses is something to be desired and, if possible, copied. However, achieving a balance of flowers and grass is not always easy.

Fritillaria meleagris The exciting spotting on the bell flower has given rise to the name snakeshead.
◗ , 25cm/10in

◆ *These flowers are excellent for grouping in a shady border or for naturalizing in grass.*

3. EARLY SUMMER

Beautiful flowers, fresh foliage and longer, warmer days combine to make this one of the loveliest of times.

COMBINING PLANTS

As SUMMER GATHERS PACE so the borders begin to fill out. Soft, pastel colours predominate and it is the arrangement of these which determines the success or otherwise of the planting schemes.

Giving careful thought to the placing of flowers (here, *Viola cornuta* and *Malva moschata alba*) will result in effects which are pleasing to the eye and which strike chords of harmony throughout the garden.

***Delphinium* 'Alice Artindale'** One of the loveliest of all delphiniums, 'Alice Artindale' possesses the most sumptuous double flowers. Place it with violet, green, even some reds. ○, 1.5m × 75cm/5 × 2½ft

Delphiniums, feverfew, salvia, viola and mallow are combined and this restful arrangement of yellow and blue tints, where the most prevalent colour is the green of the foliage, works well. The addition of tones of orange or violet would make for a less relaxed, more startling picture.

COMBINING PLANTS

EXCITING FLOWER AND LEAF COMBINATIONS may be achieved with a little trial and error. Some associations will readily suggest themselves, others will need to be worked at. Teaming copper with lime-green, purple with grey and orange with blue are just a few of the compositions to be tried. Equally successful are blue, white and silver or simply primrose and white.

Viola labradorica This moody little viola looks very effective when interplanted with silver leafed artemisias. 10 × 30cm/4in × 1ft

STAKING

Ensuring that taller-growing perennials will not collapse in wind and rain is vital if attractive borders are to be maintained.

Supporting stakes should be set around plants whilst growth is still at an early stage.

An alternative to ready-made stakes are hazel or birch twigs. Bamboo canes tied with twine will also provide adequate support. All supports will be hidden in a short while as foliage increases.

Aquilegia **'Magpie'** A sombre atmosphere is created by placing this unusual aquilegia amongst purple sage. 60 × 45cm/ 2 × 1½ft

◆ *Aquilegias come readily from seed but will frequently cross one with another.*

Viola cornuta alba Use this charming and understated viola to infill amongst other perennials. 10 × 30cm/ 4in × 1ft

Gillenia trifoliata A most graceful and unusual plant to bring life to otherwise dull areas. 1m x 60cm/ 3 x 2ft

Iris sibirica The lavender blue of this Siberian flag tones well with pale pinks. For moist soil. ○, 60 × 60cm/2 × 2ft

Erysimum 'Bowles' Mauve' This perennial wallflower looks splendid against a silver background. 60 × 60cm/2 × 2ft

Lychnis chalcedonica A difficult red to place outside a hot scheme. Look out for the double form. 1m × 45cm/3 × 1½ft

Thermopsis montana Straw-yellow flower closely resembles that of a lupin. The plant has a tendency to run. 75 × 75cm/2½ × 2½ft

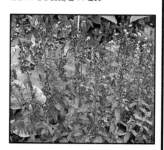

Veronica austriaca 'Shirley Blue' Drift this sprawling plant throughout a yellow and blue border. ○, 20 × 30cm/8in × 1ft

Alchemilla mollis (**Lady's mantle**) Lime-green flowers over clumps of slightly glaucous leaves which hold the raindrops in a most appealing manner. 60 × 60cm/2 × 2ft

Diascia vigilis Put this pretty pink with the silver-grey foliage of lamb's ears *Stachys byzantina* 'Silver Carpet'. ○, 45 × 60cm/1½ x 2ft

Baptisia australis The false indigo is a worthwhile plant to seek out and include in a blue scheme. 75 × 60cm/ 2½ × 2ft

Geranium phaeum Named the mourning widow. Cut back after flowering to encourage a second show. ◑, 75 × 45cm/2½ × 1½ft

113

BEDDING OUT

RECENT YEARS HAVE SEEN A REVIVAL of formal bedding schemes where massed plants make for eye-catching displays. The large number of plants required can mostly be raised from seed. Informal use of bedding plants also provides some bright splashes during the duller months.

Nigella Love-in-the-mist creates an ephemeral effect when allowed to drift through the border.
○, 45cm/1½ft

Nemesia Easily grown, nemesia is quick to flower in a wide array of colours.
○, 30–45cm/1–1½ft

Limnanthes douglasii (Poached egg flower) Edge a border with this sunny little flower which is loved by bees. ○, 15cm/6in

Salvia splendens There is nothing understated about the many red varieties of this permanently popular annual. ○, 30cm/1ft

Nicotiana Intensely fragrant at dusk, nicotiana (the tobacco flower) should be grown near a path where its perfume may be appreciated.
○, 30–90 × 30–45cm/ 1–3 × 1-1½ft

Felicia amelloides Plant the blue marguerite in groups to fill any spaces left in sunny borders.
○, 45 × 30cm/1½ × 1ft

MANY OF THE PLANT COMBINATIONS used in parks and public gardens, where bedding out is a seasonal task, can readily be adapted to the beds and borders of the smaller garden. Alternatively, pots and tubs can be filled with dramatic results.

Petunia F1 hybrids will give a constant succession of flowers from planting out until the frosts.
○, 15–45cm/6in–1½ft

Heliotrope Somewhat less commonly used today than in the past, heliotrope (or cherry pie) is strongly perfumed. ○, 45cm/1½ft

Pelargonium Zonal pelargoniums are happiest in full sun and make ideal subjects for beds or containers.
○, 45cm/1½ft

◆ *Often commonly named geranium, pelargoniums will not withstand frost.*

115

A wonderful
combination of tall
foxgloves pushing
through a bush of the
hybrid musk rose
'Penelope' on the edge
of woodland.

SOME PLANTS ARE LIKE OLD FRIENDS. Familiar, constant and reliable they have proved their worth time and time again. They are part of the garden tradition and it would be difficult to imagine flower borders without them.

***Rosa gallica* 'Camaieux'** The combination of white, pink, crimson in this old rose will excite comment. 1.5 × 1.2m/5 × 4ft

***Geranium endressii* 'Wargrave Pink'** This hardy geranium makes effective ground cover. 60 × 60cm/ 2 × 2ft

◆ *The majority of hardy geraniums will benefit from being cut hard back after flowering.*

Digitalis purpurea The foxglove is a splendid plant to include in a shady position at the back of the border. 1.2m × 30cm/4 × 1ft

Lilium martagon Of all the species this is possibly best known with its turban-shaped flowers. The form shown here is *L. m. album*. ◑ 1.5 × 30cm/5 × 1ft

Lupinus polyphyllus Russell lupins are amongst the brightest of the early summer flowers. ○, 1.2m × 45cm/4 × 1½ft

◆ *A number of distinct colours are in cultivation: 'Limelight', 'Vogue' and 'Magnificence'.*

***Nepeta* 'Six Hills Giant'** Deep blue flowers and silvery leaves make this a very attractive plant. ○, 60 × 60cm/2 × 2ft

OLD-FASHIONED FLOWERS

***Paeonia lactiflora* 'Sarah Bernhardt'** Double, soft pink flowers with the appearance in texture of crumpled tissue paper. 1 × 1m/3 × 3ft

GROWING PEONIES

Peonies are suitable for planting in sun or light shade. Crowns should be placed fairly close to the surface of the soil. If placed too deeply, then they will flower less freely.

Peonies prefer rich, heavy, well-drained soil which remains moist during summer months. They will grow better if given some form of support.

They resent disturbance.

Polemonium reptans The blue Jacob's ladder will, if left, gently seed around. 30 × 45cm/1 × 1½ft

***Geranium pratense* 'Mrs Kendall Clark'** A charming geranium which fits into many colour schemes. 60 × 60cm/2 x 2ft

Lunaria annua Strictly speaking a biennial, honesty is most often grown for its pearly seed pods. ◑, 75 × 30cm/2½ × 1ft

Scabiosa caucasica The flowers of this scabious are a pretty addition to the early summer scene. ○, 60 × 60cm/2 × 2ft

***Centaurea montana* 'Alba'** This form of cornflower will respond to division every three years. 45 × 60cm/ 1½ × 2ft

Crambe cordifolia Wonderful sprays of frothy, scented white flowers for the back of the border. ○, 2 × 1.2m/6 × 4ft

Hesperis matronalis Although short-lived the scented sweet rocket will usually self-seed. ◑, 75 x 60cm/2½ x 2ft

Aquilegia vulgaris A true cottage-garden plant, the columbine has attractive grey-green leaves. ◑, 75 × 45cm/2½ × 1½ft

BROAD BEDS OF FLAG IRIS and long peony borders capture the imagination now. As flowers fade and dead heads are removed, attractive foliage maintains interest in terms of form and texture. It is worth keeping the flower beds tidy and neat so that shapes can be appreciated.

OLD-FASHIONED FLOWERS

Flag irises enjoy a situation where their creeping rhizomes can be sun-baked. Here they are shown with gladiolus.

◆ *Lift irises such as these and divide every few years.*

4. MIDSUMMER

Summer days bring warm, sunny hours.
Burgeoning flower borders reach peaks
of perfection.

SUMMER SCENTS

CONTINUITY OF BLOOM

As the season progresses early-flowering plants, including many of the spring bulbs, will have finished blooming and have died down. To achieve continuity and a well furnished look, these gaps must be filled. In many cases the later-flowering perennials will reach maturity to obscure vacant spaces. Additionally annuals, such as centaurea, clarkia and the deliciously scented stocks, mathiola, can be introduced. These will flower right up until the first of the winter frosts.

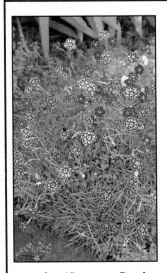

Dianthus **'Gravetye Gem'** All the pinks enjoy an open, free draining site. ○, E, 20 × 30cm/8in × 1ft

Dianthus **'Pike's Pink'** A delightful subject for the rock garden or front of border. ○, E, 15 × 15cm/ 6 × 6in

Iris graminea **(Plum tart iris)** Flowers, smelling of cooked plums, nestle well down amongst the leaves. ◑, 30cm × 30cm/1 × 1ft

Lilium candidum Heavily scented flowers in purest white make the Madonna lily an outstanding subject. ○, 1.2m/4ft

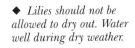
◆ *Lilies should not be allowed to dry out. Water well during dry weather.*

Lilium **'Uchida'** Charmingly marked. This lily would be equally at home in a container. ○, 1.2m/4ft

MIDSUMMER AIR IS PERFUMED WITH BEWITCHING SCENTS carried on gentle breezes. Bees murmur throughout long, dreamy days and borders are overrun with fragrant blooms. Now is the moment to linger, to delight in the riches of an unfolding, changing landscape.

Monarda **'Cambridge Scarlet'** It is the leaves of the bergamots which are so strongly aromatic.
○, 1 × 1m/3 × 3ft

Origanum laevigatum. In common with most herbs, marjoram thrives in a sunny spot. 60 × 60cm/2 × 2ft

Lavandula No garden should be without generous clumps of sweet-smelling lavender. ○, 60 × 60cm+/2 × 2ft+

◆ *Clip lavenders hard back in the spring to retain healthy, vigorous plants.*

SUMMER SCENTS

EVENING HEIGHTENS THE HEADY SCENT OF LILIES grown in the open ground or grouped in pots. Lavenders spill out onto paths, their fragrance familiar and nostalgic. Tobacco flowers release exotic aromas as twilight gathers.

Lathyrus odoratus is the original sweet pea. Over the years the range of colours has greatly increased.
○, 30cm–2.4m/1–8ft

CULTIVATING SWEET PEAS

Young plants should be set out in prepared soil containing plentiful amounts of compost or manure.

Train plants to grow up a supporting structure. In the border bean-sticks or bamboo canes are perfectly satisfactory.

Tie in tendrils to supports and water well in periods of dry weather. Remove all spent flowers to ensure a continuous succession of blooms.

Cosmos atrosanguineus (Chocolate cosmos) Unbelievably smelling of hot chocolate, this plant is a must. Suitable for a pot.
○, 75 × 45cm/2½ × 1½ft

Lathyrus rotundifolius Flowers of brick-red make this a most unusual perennial pea. 1.8m/6ft

Phlox **'Fujiyama'** A handsome plant with large heads of pure white which are pleasantly scented.
○, 1m × 75cm/3 × 2½ft

Phlox **'Norah Leigh'** Lilac flowers are carried above prettily variegated leaves.
○, 75 × 60cm/2½ × 2ft

Hemerocallis lilioasphodelus **(H. flava)** This day lily is scented. Removal of dead heads prolongs flowering.
75 × 75cm/2½ × 2½ft

Nicotiana The enticing fragrance of tobacco plants will fill an enclosed space.
○, 30–90 × 30–45cm/1–3 × 1–1½ft

◆ *Nicotiana is best treated as a half-hardy annual and raised from seed each year. It is shown here behind a mist of gypsophila.*

125

Mown grass acts as a quiet foil to a diversity of flower tints. Taller growing phlox and campanulas hold sway at the back of the border. Mound-forming clumps and plants which trail hug the ground to add intimacy and variety.

CAREFULLY ORCHESTRATED BORDERS of complementary flowers and foliage are the outstanding feature of the season. Plants closely packed together bestow a wonderful sense of fullness and, on a practical note, deny weeds the opportunity for growth.

Rosa **'Graham Thomas'** This new English rose associates beautifully with deep blue delphinium. ○, 1.5 × 1m/5 × 3ft

Alstroemeria **'Ligtu Hybrids'** The eye is drawn towards the soft pink alstroemerias in this scheme. ○, 60 × 30cm/2 × 1ft

Geranium psilostemon and *Geranium* **'Johnson's Blue'** These two hardy geraniums create a dramatic effect when placed together. 60 × 60cm/2 × 2ft

◆ *Bright colours are here toned down with the silver-leafed stachys.*

127

A LIVING TAPESTRY

LOOKING AHEAD

Now is an ideal time in which to plan alterations to the flower garden. A critical look at the borders will show up those plants which perform badly, those which have outgrown their allocated space and those whose colours clash. Intended changes may be noted down in readiness for the autumn when plants may be lifted, divided and moved.

Argyranthemum '**Jamaica Primrose'** A most appealing tender marguerite for a warm spot. ○, 1 × 1m/ 3 × 3ft

Stachys macrantha is distinctive for its purplish-pink flowers. A good front-of-border plant. 45 × 45cm/1½ × 1½ft

Eryngium variifolium The steely blue flower-heads of this sea-holly are rounded and spiky. ○, 45 × 25cm/ 1½ft × 10in

Campanula poscharskyana This rockery campanula will quickly spread to cover a wide area. 25 × 60cm/ 10in × 2ft

Campanula pyramidalis A giant Canterbury bell. Plant this to tower through and above old roses. ○, 1.2m × 60cm/4 × 2ft

Lychnis coronaria A striking plant although the magenta flowers sometimes make it difficult to place. ○, 45 × 45cm/1½ × 1½ft

Salvia nemorosa '**East Friesland'** Deep purple flowers are shown off against the golden foliage of neighbouring herbs. ○, 45 × 45cm/1½ × 1½ft

◆ *Once established the perennial salvias should remain undisturbed without periodic division.*

PLANTING IN BLOCKS OF COLOUR is a way of giving an effective structure to the herbaceous border. Whites, blues, lemons and creams on the outside edges; towards the centre pastel pinks to deeper shades of carmine, fiery reds and oranges crowned with purples and mauves.

A LIVING TAPESTRY

Thalictrum aquilegiifolium (Meadow rue) Fluffy pink flowers create a sense of lightness and airiness. 75 × 60cm/2½ × 2ft

***Penstemon* 'Chester Scarlet'** There is nothing uncertain about this scarlet. Penstemons may be increased by taking cuttings. ○, 60 × 45cm/2 × 1½ft

Hemerocallis Clumps of red and orange day lilies convey the full heat of summer in this hot border. 1 × 1m/ 3 × 3ft

Acanthus spinosissimus Purple-tipped bracts in elegant spikes make this a plant of distinction. ○, 1.2m × 75cm/4 × 2½ft

Helichrysum italicum The curry plant shown with geraniums and catmint. ○, 60 × 60cm/2 × 2ft

◆ *Herbs need not be confined to the kitchen garden. They often make good association plants.*

A Living Tapestry

SUCCESSFUL FLOWER DISPLAYS are the result of much thought and effort. Combinations are carefully considered and awareness is given to leaf form as well as to the colour of individual blooms. Some factors cannot be judged, but if you know your plants and local conditions you can achieve spectacular results.

Astrantia major involucrata Even as the flowers of the masterwort die they continue to look interesting. ◑, 60 × 60cm/2 × 2ft

Campanula lactiflora must be one of the mainstays of the summer border. 1.2m × 60cm/4 × 2ft

Monarda didyma **'Croftway Pink'** (Bergamot) Seen here against the violet-blue of nepeta, to good effect. 1m × 45cm/3 × 1½ft

Linum narbonense settles happily amongst the paving stones where its roots enjoy a cool run. ○, 45 × 30cm/ 1½ × 1ft

Geranium sanguineum **striatum** at the front of the border to give a full, informal effect. 30 × 45cm/ 1 × 1½ft

Eremurus bungei Conspicuous foxtail lilies dominate plants in a border giving height and interest. ○, 1.5m × 60cm/5 × 2ft

Geranium himalayense **'Plenum'** Lilac double flowers ensure the popularity of this appealing plant. 60 × 60cm/2 × 2ft

![A living tapestry border photograph]

***Achillea filipendulina* 'Gold Plate'** Bold clumps of yarrow add form to a carefully planned hot border. ○, 1.5m × 60cm/ 5 × 2ft

◆ *The flat-heads of yarrow are effective when seen against a plant with spires of flowers, like salvia.*

A Living Tapestry

DARE TO GROW DIASCIAS

These exceedingly pretty, mainly pink garden plants have increased in popularity in recent years. However, an undeserved reputation for tenderness precludes their inclusion in many garden schemes. Given moist conditions with good drainage to minimize winter wet, they should survive, particularly if cutting back is delayed until mid-spring. All are easy to propagate from basal cuttings.

Lysimachia punctata A colourful border plant but one with a tendency to spread beyond bounds. 75 × 75cm/2½ × 2½ft

Dictamnus albus purpureus Slow to establish but well worth taking trouble over. 60 × 60cm/2 × 2ft

***Hemerocallis* 'Bonanza'** Deep yellow flowers which bloom much of the summer if dead headed. 1 × 1m/ 3 × 3ft

Diascia rigescens Sprawling spikes of pink flowers will last throughout the summer. ○, 30 × 45cm/1 × 1½ft

AMONGST THE LOVELIEST and most desirable of summer flowers are those which will not withstand frost. Less-hardy plants make excellent subjects for pots and containers. Grouped together on a terrace or beside a door they can form an attractive feature. Brugmansias, cannas and a phormium dominate this display.

Fuchsia '**Thalia**' Dark, velvet leaves show off many hanging trumpets of scarlet. Propagate from cuttings. ○, 45 × 45cm/1½ × 1½ft

Gazania South African daisies, available in a whole range of colours, make for an intense show. ◐, 30 × 20cm/1ft × 8in

Brugmansia (Angel's trumpet, datura) An excellent plant for a pot. Here, the long, white hanging trumpets look coolly elegant. ◯, 1.2 x 1m/4 x 3ft

Felicia amelloides The flowers of the blue marguerite are appealing when teamed with the palest of lemon yellows. ◯, 45 x 30cm/1½ x 1ft

TENDER PERENNIALS

COMBAT COLD

Many of these tender perennials will survive the winter provided they are given a frost-free place. Grow them in pots throughout the colder months and then transfer to the open ground for the gardening season. Repot as the temperature falls.

Hedychium coccineum **'Tara'** Brilliant tangerine spikes contribute a feeling of hot, exotic climes to the summer border. ◯, 1.2 × 1m/4 × 3ft

◆ *For a more subtle scheme, try* Hedychium flavescens *which is pale yellow and scented.*

Tender Perennials

Lobelia syphilitica These elegant blue spires would enhance most situations. Soil should be kept moist. 1.2m × 30cm/4 × 1ft

Lobelia tupa Spectacular in flower. This lobelia requires really good drainage and protection from winter wet. ○, 1.2m × 30cm/4 × 1ft

Eucomis bicolor The quiet charm of the green-flowered pineapple plant requires a warm spot. ○, 45 × 60cm/1½ × 2ft

Dahlia merckii A beautiful and graceful tuberous plant. Very different from the ordinary run of dahlias. ○, 90 × 60cm/3 × 2ft

Summer Bulbs

In addition to this dahlia it is worth seeking out other bulbs for the mid-season. For something different try *Tigridia pavonia, Ixia* and the dwarf *Rhodohypoxis*.

Gladiolus hybrid Possibly these tall, rather stiff flower spikes are at their best in a formal bedding scheme. ○, 1.2m × 30cm/4 × 1ft

Salvia discolor Absolutely outstanding. Indigo-black flowers above white-felted leaves. Keep frost free. ○, 60 × 30cm/2 × 1ft

Salvia uliginosa Adds grace later in the summer. Protect new shoots of the bog sage from slugs. ○, 2m × 45cm/ 6 × 1½ft

Given a little protection, many of the plants thought likely to succumb to frost will come through a cold winter. A sheet of glass, dying ferns or bracken placed across the plant's crown is often enough to ensure survival.

Salvia patens The beautiful bright blue flowers are produced on the branches all summer to autumn. ○, 60 × 45cm/2 × 1½ft

Lobelia cardinalis **'Queen Victoria'** Deep wine red leaves and stems and intense red flowers dominate this striking plant. ○, 90 × 30cm/3 × 1ft

◆ *Surprisingly this foliage and flower looks superb when set against orange.*

5. LATE SUMMER/ AUTUMN

Borders are ablaze with the rich hues of autumn as the Flower Garden moves into a new and thrilling season.

A Late Show

As summer draws to a close the autumn flowers come into their own. Exciting kniphofias, fiery crocosmias and late-flowering salvias ensure an interesting and continuous display.

Dahlia **'Gerrie Hoek'** This intense pink associates well with pink Japanese anemones. ○, 60 × 60cm/ 2 × 2ft.

Crocosmia **'Lucifer'**, *Dahlia* **'Bishop of Llandaff'** Placed together these two late flowering plants bring excitement to the border. ○

◆ *Dahlia tubers should be lifted in the autumn and stored in a frost-free place.*

An Herbaceous Clematis

Clematis heracleifolia Grow this non-climbing clematis for its sky blue, scented flowers. Delay cutting back and tidying the dead stems until the spring. 1m × 75cm/3 × 2½ft.

Kniphofia caulescens This striking poker has interesting grey-green, serrated leaves. ○, 1m × 60cm/3 × 2ft

Macleaya microcarpa Allow plenty of space for this dramatic perennial. 2 × 1m/6 × 3ft.

Easy to Grow

Persicaria campanulata Until the first frosts the red stems of this persicaria remain an outstanding feature at the back of the border. 1 × 1m/3 × 3ft.

GLOWING COLOURS typify the time of year. A last rose ('Just Joey'), the flat yellow heads of achillea and generous clumps of crocosmias and dahlias maintain interest throughout the garden. In the foreground the crimson tassels of amaranthus (Love-lies-bleeding) elegantly sweep to the ground.

A Late Show

A Late Show

Boldly planted clumps of late-flowering perennials contribute a sense of drama to the borders. Far from fading, these autumn tints are rich, lustrous and full of purpose. Not least are the lovely cultivars of *Anemone hybrida*, the Japanese anemones.

Dahlia 'Grenadier'
Tuberous dahlias dress up an end of season border. ○, 60 × 60cm/2 × 2ft.

Tidying the Borders

Frequent dead heading, the cutting down of spent plants and a light forking over of the ground keep the borders trim and in shape.

Without Equal

Amongst the many available cultivars of **Anemone hybrida** are **'Hadspen Abundance'**, a deep purplish pink, **'Honorine Jobert'**, a large white, or **'Königin Charlotte'**, the best of the mid-pinks. 1.5m/5ft.

◆ *All the Japanese anemones have an extended flowering period. Cut back as the flowers fade.*

Phygelius × rectus **'Salmon Leap'** Treat this shrub as a perennial and cut back when the flowers are over. 1 × 1m/3 × 3ft.

Crinum powellii These beautiful, fragrant flowers are effective against a sunny wall. ○, 1m × 60cm/3 × 2ft.

♦ *Crinums are not difficult to grow but like a rich, well drained soil.*

Crocosmia 'Mount Usher' No garden should be without a selection of these perennials. ○, 60 × 30cm/ 2 × 1ft.

Kirengeshoma palmata A plant for moist ground close to water. ◑, 1m × 75cm/3 × 2½ft.

Fuchsia magellanica 'Gracilis Variegata' A graceful shrub with slender crimson-purple flowers. 75 × 75cm/2½ × 2½ft.

ELEGANT AND UNUSUAL

Salvia × *sylvestris* 'Indigo' Mass together spires of this dark-flowered salvia for a beautiful and dramatic border statement. ○, 60 × 45cm/2 × 1½ft.

Agapanthus 'Loch Hope' Amongst the most magnificent of dark blue forms of African lily. ○, 1.2m × 75cm/4 × 2½ft.

Aconitum carmichaelii Roots of Monkshood, or Wolf's bane, are poisonous. 1.5m × 30cm/5 × 1ft.

Liriope muscari Tiny spikes of violet flowers are sometimes masked by the leaves. 30 × 45cm/1 × 1½ft.

DAZZLING DAISIES

DAISY-TYPE FLOWERS dominate the late summer borders together with chrysanthemums and dahlias. These heavily petalled blooms enliven the last days of summer.

A MINIATURE DAISY

Aster thompsonii **'Nanus'**
Continuously in flower from mid-summer, this little aster is an invaluable garden plant. Place in a sunny spot and leave undisturbed.
45 × 25cm/1½ft × 10in.

Aster × frikartii **'Mönch'** A long flowering period makes this a highly regarded daisy. ◯,
75 × 45cm/2½ × 1½ft.

Aster novi-belgii
'Beechwood Charm' Warm, vibrant flowers lighten drear days. ◯,
1.2m × 45cm/4 × 1½ft.

Aster novi-belgii **'Goliath'**
Regular division in spring results in freer flowering plants. ◯, 1.2m × 45cm/
4 × 1½ft.

Aster novi-belgii **'Lilac Time'**, *Aster novi-belgii* **'Jenny'** These asters form a pleasing composition. ◯

◆ *Taller growing asters require some form of staking. Hazel sticks are ideal.*

Aster novi-belgii **'Winston Churchill'** Silver-grey foliage is a marvellous foil for these flowers. ◯,
75 × 45cm/2½ × 1½ft.

MICHAELMAS DAISIES are the grandees of all late flowering perennials. The flowers of the various species cover a broad spectrum and plants will prosper in most situations. In the past asters have been prone to mildew; many disease resistant strains are now available.

DAZZLING DAISIES

Clumps of dwarf asters hug the front of the border backed by those of taller stature. The introduction at intervals of white flowers helps to carry the eye forwards.

◆ *The scale of this late summer border may easily be adapted to fit a smaller space.*

DAZZLING DAISIES

ALONGSIDE ASTERS, dendranthema (as chrysanthemums have been renamed), heleniums, helianthus, and rudbeckias all contribute their daisy flowers to the warm glow of the autumnal borders. As the sun lowers so these tints are picked up and given greater intensity.

SHOW STOPPER

***Dendranthema* 'Corngold'**
Dendranthema such as this one make a bold statement. Specifically grown for cutting or show they are best given some form of protection from wind and rain. ○, 1.2m/4ft.

***Dendranthema* 'Ruby Mound'** Deep ruby red flowers are tightly packed together. ○, 1.2m/4ft.

◆ *An effective association is achieved by planting deep pink dendranthema with* **Sedum 'Autumn Joy'.**

***Dendranthema* 'Nathalie'**
Named cultivars are the result of much crossing and recrossing. 90cm/3ft.

***Arctotis* × *hybrida* 'Wine'**
Treat this South African daisy as an annual in colder areas. ○, 60cm/2ft.

Rudbeckia fulgida **'Goldsturm'** These prolific yellow daisies with their black central cones seem to last for all time. Dead-heading prolongs the flowering season. ○, 75 × 45cm/ 2½ × 1½ft.

◆ *Partner* **'Goldsturm'** *with the purple daisy heads of the cone flower* **Echinacea purpurea**.

FRONT OF BORDER

Inula barbata A cheerful little subject to tuck in amongst other flowers. Petals are an unusual light, greenish yellow. ○, 60 × 45cm/2 × 1½ft.

Helianthus 'Monarch' Brilliant yellow sunflowers soar skywards above rough foliage. ○, 2.1 × 1m/ 7 × 3ft.

◆ *Grown from seed sunflowers are great favourites with children.*

Helenium **'Moerheim Beauty'** Easily grown perennial with rich mahogany flowers. ○, 1m × 60cm/3 × 2ft.

145

A S THE GARDENING YEAR DRAWS TO A CLOSE, and thoughts once more turn to spring, there is still much in the flower garden to attract attention and excite interest.

Schizostylis coccinea alba In cold areas give the crowns some over-winter protection. 60 × 30cm/ 2 × 1ft

Schizostylis coccinea 'Sunrise' Kaffir lilies continue to bloom even in low temperatures. 60 × 30cm/2 × 1ft

Sedum 'Autumn Joy' Butterflies love this sedum which remains pleasing throughout the winter. ○, 60 × 60cm/2 × 2ft

Sedum 'Ruby Glow' Crimson flowers quietly fade as the year progresses. ○, 30 × 30cm/1 × 1ft

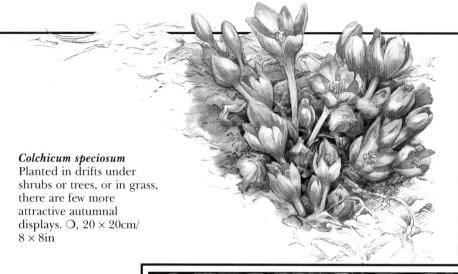

Colchicum speciosum
Planted in drifts under shrubs or trees, or in grass, there are few more attractive autumnal displays. ○, 20 × 20cm/ 8 × 8in

Enjoying partial shade, many forms of ***Tricyrtis***, toad lily, form elegant clumps through the first fallen leaves.
60 × 45cm/2 × 1½ft

Nerine bowdenii These showy South African bulbs are reliably hardy.
○, 45 × 20cm/1½ft × 8in

◆ *When planting, place bulbs on a little horticultural grit to improve drainage.*

ROSES

THE ROSE FAMILY, or *Rosa*, which is Latin for 'rose', has captured imaginations for thousands of years with its myths, legends and symbolism. Steeped in history, the rose embraces a kaleidoscope of tones in numerous exquisite flower shapes; its prickles and foliage parade a diverse range of habits unrivalled by any other plant family. Roses are classified according to these distinguishing characteristics, beginning with Wild roses and developing through history as man took up rose cultivation.

Species roses or Wild roses are native to many regions of the northern hemisphere. Their unique and distinctive features grace any place, yielding year round interest: Wild yellow roses boast elegance of habit; Sweetbriars exude richly aromatic foliage; Cinnamon roses and unusual species fascinate with peeling stems, winged thorns and bristly shoots; Dog roses charm with their simple flowers; Rugosas flaunt their ornamental hips.

Old Shrub roses are natural hybrids of Species roses. Rose breeding got under way when man collected and cultivated them. By the end of the eighteenth century Albas, Gallicas, Damasks and Moschatas prevailed, culminating in the development of Centifolias and Moss roses. Their balance of foliage and flowers is perfect and their fragrance and flower-shapes are unrivalled.

Western rose culture was revolutionized when breeders began crossing *Rosa chinensis* hybrids, introduced from the east, with Old Shrub roses. A new race of roses was born: the Autumn Damasks (Portland roses), Bourbons and Hybrid Perpetuals, which inherited the Old rose fragrance and flower-shapes, but yielded the ability to repeat-flower – virtually unknown at the time. Their distinctive appearance and flexibility of habit inspired innovative design for new rose gardens.

(*Left*) A good combination: *Viola cornuta alba* twines comfortably through the branches of an old moss rose. Violas thrive better if they are planted on the shady side of roses.

(*Right*) Spreading bushes of Gallica roses: the pink 'Président de Sèze' and the crimson 'Charles de Mills' notable for the quartered 'sliced off' formation of its flowers. Both roses are very scented but only once-flowering.

Modern Shrub roses are relatively recent introductions and include: Hybrid Species roses, closely related to the Species roses; famous old favourites like the Dwarf Polyanthas (Poly-Poms); the outstandingly floriferous Hybrid Musks; and recent hybrid groups such as English roses and Ground-cover roses.

Large-flowered Climbers are often climbing versions or 'sports' from a shrub or bush rose. Climbing Noisettes bear clusters of small, sweetly fragrant flowers in soft hues. Ramblers are in three groups (all fragrant) distinguished by their ancestry: Sempervirens Ramblers bear exquisite clusters of small flowers; Multiflora Ramblers have upright growth and large trusses of small flowers; and Wichuraiana Ramblers produce elegant sprays of rather larger flowers.

Modern Bush roses are the most popular roses of the twentieth century: they differ from Shrub roses in being generally short and compact, and dominated by the flowers which they bear. Vividness and brightness are key characteristics. Although many alluring hues may be found among the Floribundas (Cluster-flowered roses), and multicoloured and hand-painted effects among the Miniature and Patio roses, it is the Hybrid Teas that embody the history of man's pursuit of the perfect bloom.

Standard roses come in miniature, half and full-standard stems. Depending on the type of rose budded onto the stem, it produces a ball, mop-head or weeping-standard. Standard roses are most useful in formal gardens where they add dimension and may be used to 'float the eye' across massed plantings.

The Dwarf Polyantha (or Poly-Pom) rose, 'Francine Austin', grown as a standard.

SITING

When choosing roses the site should be the principal consideration. There are certain conditions which roses will not tolerate: dense shade, waterlogged ground, poor soil, soil which has a high lime content, and soil which has already been growing roses.

An exposed site is best suited to Rugosas or Scotch briars, whereas Dwarf Polyanthas (Poly-Poms), China roses and English roses need enclosure and protection. Dog roses, Wild Yellow roses, Sweetbriars, Cinnamon roses and Albas mostly tolerate semi-shade, suiting woodland plantings as well as wild gardens, where Ramblers can soar up into trees or smother secret arbours. Large, open or moderately exposed spaces can be broken up with informal groups of giant Hybrid Species roses, while carpets and cascades of Ground-cover roses can colour the vista. Damasks, Centifolias and Hybrid Musks make excellent floriferous, fragrant screens and hedges to protect the mixed borders of the inner garden, which must abound with Gallicas, Moss Roses, Autumn Damasks, Bourbons and Hybrid Perpetuals. Arches and pergolas used to line walkways create controlled vistas festooned with Climbing Noisettes and Ramblers. Large-flowered Climbers are best suited to wall and trellis.

It would be true to say Hybrid Teas and Floribundas look out of place among Old Shrub roses – better in a bed of their own. Although many smaller Old Shrub roses do grow successfully in pots – they should not be positioned beside Miniatures in a tiny patio or courtyard!

Propagation and Timing

Traditionally roses were 'budded' in the field onto 'rootstocks' and lifted in autumn, after they had been hardened-off by frost, to be sold bare-rooted while they were still in their dormant state. They were thus planted in autumn – before nurserymen put them in containers for sale all year round. Keen gardeners always rushed to plant then, to catch the warmth in the soil and get them going before atrocious winters set in. Very sensible! Their roses had all winter and spring to get watered-in and properly established ready for a magnificent show in summer.

The advent of container roses has encouraged wider use of 'cuttings', which has the advantage of no 'suckers' (see below) – attractive particularly to the large scale landscaper. 'Bench-grafting' under glass hastens the production line for commercial breeders as well as making propagation of non-hardy varieties possible.

Some varieties of roses lend themselves to 'layering' (pinning a stem in the soil to form roots and thus a new plant) and 'division' as successful self-propagating methods. Only first generation Species roses will come true from seed.

Planting

Apart from considerations of the height and spread of a rose, spacing is a matter of design: 'How dense do you want them?'

Planting An Individual Rose Have to hand a barrow of 'organic matter' comprised of well-rotted horse manure, mixed with peat or cocoa-fibre and three handfuls of bonemeal

'Cornelia' is one of the best of the scented and long-flowering hybrid musk roses. The white St Bernard's lily (*Anthericum liliago*) grows in front, enjoying the same conditions, sun and well-drained soil, as the rose.

or the like. Prepare a hole at least 60cm/2ft diameter by digging out the topsoil to a depth of about 23cm/9in and put it to one side – use a polythene sheet. Break up 23cm/9in subsoil in the bottom of the hole, and discard about half, replacing with and incorporating organic matter. Put some of the topsoil back into the hole working in more organic matter to a nice friable mixture forming a mound in the centre. Place the plant into the hole, spreading the roots out over the

(Left) The wonderful once-flowering modern rose 'Constance Spry', which has the rare scent of myrrh. Normally grown as a lax shrub, its display is even more sumptuous here as a climber trained on a wall.

(Right) A mixed bed of shrub roses and foxgloves: the crimson 'Gipsy Boy', the pink Centifolia rose 'De Meaux' and the small perennial foxglove, *Digitalis lutea*.

mound (or carefully remove the container) so that the 'union' (where the shoots and roots join) is 2.5cm/1in–5cm/2in below the ground level – allowing for settlement. Work the rest of the topsoil and organic matter back into the hole round the roots, firming well as you go. Water well and mulch, to preserve moisture and keep the soil active. Roses planted during spring and summer should be kept watered until established.

Planting A Bed of Roses The soil preparation itself is best done in advance, i.e. 'double-digging' or digging to two spade depths. Don't discard any subsoil as this is unnecessary unless finished levels are crucial.

Pests and Diseases It is true some roses are less prone to diseases than others but including them in a routine spraying programme will do no harm. Rust, blackspot and mildew pose the greatest threats and as in most things prevention is better than cure. During the dormant season apply tar-wash (Phenol), and as soon as the leaves emerge commence two-weekly applications of fungicide (Myclo-butanil) for the first half of summer (then change it). Pay particular attention to the undersides of leaves. Treat harmful blackfly with pesticide (Primicarb) which may be combined with most fungicides. It is also worthwhile including concentrated seaweed extract.

been grafted or 'budded'. The consequence is sapping of the strength of the rose and ultimately takeover or 'reversion'. Suckers are easily recognizable by their vigorous erect stems, and Dog rose type flowers and foliage. They grow from below the graft or union, from whence they should be removed. To cut them off won't suffice – they'll thrive on the experience. Rather, they must be torn off at the point where they shoot from the rootstock.

PRUNING

Principles Rose pruning on anything other than Hybrid Teas and Floribundas is a very controversial topic. The prime purpose of it is, and will always be, to stimulate growth, to maintain shape, and to train. It can be carried out in summer after flowering, as well as in winter. Pruning removes twiggy, old or dead branches and shortens others. It can be executed radically or with minute precision (never mind the principles!) according to the personality of the gardener.

Pruning Methods To trim and shape, reduce canes or amputate the previous season's growth, make a cut angled away from a bud. Use sharp secateurs. To remove old or dead branches, make an angled cut down to the base. Use a pruning saw.

For mass amputation, use a hedge-trimmer or shears.

Hand-cuts should always be clean. Ragged and torn edges look atrocious, but a beautifully executed radical pruning operation looks a treat. Mechanical pruning is a godsend, but afterwards take a holiday until the leaves emerge!

Feeding In early spring after pruning, established roses will thank you for a handful of bonemeal or the like raked into the surface of the soil and a thick mulching with well-rotted horse manure. Repeat in midsummer, after dead-heading, particularly on varieties which repeat-flower.

Dead-heading The removal of spent flowers encourages production of new flowering shoots on repeat-flowering roses. Make the cut above the second or third leaf below the truss or flower stem. Leave roses with ornamental hips.

Suckers These are breakthroughs of the parent plant or rootstock onto which a rose has

1. Species Roses (Wild Roses)

*Fine, large, naturally elegant shrubs –
bearing unique and distinctive stems,
thorns, foliage and hips. Their
charming fresh single flowers are
harbingers of the rose season!*

Top down: **'Stanwell Perpetual'** (Scotch briar), *Rosa villosa* **'Duplex'**, **'Mary Queen of Scots'**, and right **'Lady Penzance'** (Sweetbriar). Sweetbriars, Scotch briars and Dog roses tumble together. *Rosa eglanteria* was a favourite in medieval gardens grown alongside Old Shrub roses such as Albas, Gallicas and Damasks.

DOG ROSES (*ROSA CANINA*), WHICH GRACE SUMMER HEDGEROWS with extrovert displays of their numerous variants; Sweetbriars (*Rosa eglanteria*), famous for their apple-scented foliage which fills the air, especially after rain; and Scotch briars (*Rosa pimpinellifolia*), thriving in exposed windy sites, glowing with their bronze-tinted miniature foliage and numerous small, scented, sweet flowers – are all wild roses.

DOG ROSES *and* BRIARS

Rosa complicata (*Rosa canina* × *Rosa gallica* hybrid) Large, flat, single shocking-pink flowers with pale cream eye and golden boss. Good as a hedge. 1.5 × 2m/5 × 6ft

Rosa canina 'Andersonii' Deep, brilliant rose-pink variant of the Dog rose. Light green glaucous stems and tough downy grey-green foliage. Rich raspberry fragrance. 2 × 2.4m/6 × 8ft

Rosa pimpinellifolia (The Scotch Burnett Rose) A low-growing spreading shrub, ideal for ground cover, thriving in poor conditions. Single white flowers borne in profusion. 1 × 1m/3 × 3ft.

157

WILD YELLOW ROSES

AS IF CONTRAPUNTAL TO WINTER'S 'YELLOW FLUSH', the Wild yellow roses hail their unique golden chorus as harbingers of the rose season, triumphant that it is now early summer! The textured stems are in keeping with the diverse habit of each species which typically bears small fern-like foliage, yellow flowers and occasionally hips.

'Cantabrigiensis' ('The Cambridge Rose') Elegant upright habit – bristly brown stems with fern-like foliage turning bronze. Primrose-yellow flowers followed by bright orange-red hips. 2.2 × 2m/7 × 6ft

Rosa hugonis A graceful shrub – almost thornless, bearing tiny fern-like foliage with small, cupped primrose-yellow flowers arranged along its airy, arching, wiry twigs. 2.2 × 2m/7 × 6ft

'Canary Bird' (above and left) Bright canary-yellow single flowers, smooth red-brown stems with soft-green, dainty fern-like foliage. Very early with a second crop in late summer. 2.2 × 2.2m/7 × 7ft

◆ *'Canary Bird' is often grown as a standard rose.*

158

STRIKING FEATURES OTHER THAN FLOWERS, such as stems, thorns and foliage are useful for creating interesting textures and focal points in a mixed border, wild garden and hedge. Aromatic foliage discloses the presence of Cinnamon roses, and the brightness of sumptuous shining ornamental hips ends the rose season with a chorus, as the birds commence their banquet!

Rosa roxburghii ('Chestnut Rose') Large, single pink flowers with white centres and bright golden stamens. 2.2 × 2.2m/7 × 7ft

Rosa glauca (*Rosa rubrifolia*) Maroon bloom-covered stems with glaucous foliage. Clusters of small pink flowers with white eye. 2 × 1.2m/6 × 4ft

***Rosa moyesii* 'Geranium'** Glowing single blood-red flowers with golden-yellow stamens, borne along arching upright thorny stems. 2.4 × 2.2m/8 × 7ft

***Rosa californica* 'Plena'** Dark-pink semi-double flowers. 2.4 × 2.1m/8 × 7ft

◆ *This dense upright shrub makes a good specimen planting.*

RUGOSA ROSES

THE WILD ROSES OF JAPAN. Sturdy, stocky bushes with bright green luxuriant foliage with deeply veined leaves and large richly fragrant, tissue-textured flowers in early summer. Huge, round, orangey-red hips often coincide with intermittent mid to late summer crops. Excellent shrubs in the border, as hedging or specimens. They withstand poor soil conditions, exposed sites and are disease resistant.

'Agnes' Large blooms amid quite small, pewter grey-green leaves. Very thorny growth. 1.5 × 1.2m/5 × 4ft

'Fimbriata' ('Phoebe's Frilled Pink') Clusters of small pale pink fimbriated (frilled) flowers with darker pink and white tones. Soft light-green foliage. Few thorns. 1 × 1m/3 × 3ft

Autumn planted bare-root roses establish better with winter's own rain and stand up to late spring frosts. Order early direct from the grower!

'Blanc Double de Coubert' Large, open semi-double, pure-white blooms, of delicate tissue paper texture. 1.5 × 1.2m/5 × 4ft

◆ *This rose is exceptionally fragrant and flowers most of the summer.*

'Fru Dagmar Hastrup' Deep pink buds opening to single rose-pink flowers with conspicuous creamy stamens. 1.2 × 1.2m/4 × 4ft

'Moje Hammarberg' Large, very fragrant flowers produced freely throughout summer. 1.2 × 1m/4 × 3ft

At the back of this planting, **'Sarah van Fleet'**, **'Moje Hammarberg'** and *Salvia nemerosa* 'Superba', and in the foreground **'Fimbriata'** and *Pulmonaria saccharata* 'Alba'. A shapely, apparently deep border/hedge. Contrasting tones, textures and forms keep the eye busy, never fathoming the actual depth of the border.

RUGOSA ROSES

'Sarah van Fleet' Clusters of semi-double, cool mallow-pink tinged with lilac, flowers. Richly fragrant and very perpetual. Large luxuriant foliage. Makes a beautiful hedge. Prone to rust. 1.5 × 1m/5 × 3ft

Most Rugosas require little skilful maintenance beyond trimming to shape in winter – as hard as you like to; but trim Grootendorsts very hard.

Planting deeply (so that the 'union' is 2.5cm/1in–5cm/2in below ground level) discourages 'suckers', and prevents 'rocking' on a windy exposed site.

Bountiful hips often coincide with the second and third crops of flowers – be sure not to dead-head these varieties!

'Mrs Anthony Waterer' An arching vigorous bush massed with fragrant semi-double flowers mainly in summer. 1.2 × 1.5m/4 × 5ft

'Pink Grootendorst' Tinted salmon in bud, opening to striking rose-pink, small fimbriated flowers, borne in clusters. 1.2 × 1m/4 × 3ft

Rosa rugosa **'Alba'** Large single, silky, pure-white flowers. Blooms intermittently throughout summer. 2 × 2m/6 × 6ft

'Roseraie de l'Haÿ' Beautifully pointed buds opening to richly scented, fully double flowers of rich crimson-purple. Bright healthy foliage and fine autumn colouring. 2 × 1.5m/6 × 5ft

'Scabrosa' A compact leafy shrub bearing very large, single, light crimson-mauve flowers with creamy stamens, followed by enormous orange-red hips. Recurrent flowering. 1.5 × 1.2m/5 × 4ft

As the season of 'mellow fruitfulness' autumn is naturally equipped with dramatic stage sets and lighting for the final dance! Turgid clusters of bright red rose hips will dazzle us against a brilliant blue sky, glow seductively by the low golden-red autumn sunlight which sinks so fast, and twinkle like treasure along boughs laden with snow.

Rosa rugosa **'Alba'**

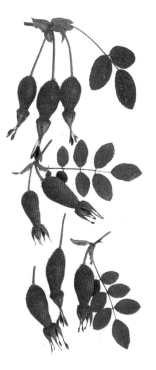

Rosa moyesii

'Robbie Burns'

Rosa × wintoniensis

Rosa glauca

Rosa villosa

Rosa roxburghii

2. OLD SHRUB ROSES (SUMMER FLOWERING)

Forerunners as garden shrubs for perfect composition of foliage and flowers; unrivalled among all roses for fragrance and flower shapes.

In the background white foxgloves and angelicas mingle with *Rosa* **'Mundi'** and **'Charles de Mills'**, whilst in the foreground **'Empress Josephine'** sits amongst purple sage and lavender. Versatile Gallicas were traditionally grown alongside herbs in the apothecary's garden.

ROSA GALLICA DATES BACK TO THE TWELFTH CENTURY B.C. to the Medes and Persians, and it was the first rose to be cultivated in the Middle East. The Romans brought it to Europe where it became the principal parent of the Old Shrub roses. Tough spreading shrubs thriving under the poorest conditions but not in shade. Solitary, upheld, very double richly fragrant blooms in exotic hues of crimson purple and maroon.

GALLICA ROSES

'Duc de Guiche' Globular flowers of crimson-magenta with purple veins and stripes – quartered with green eye. Spreading arching branches with dark foliage. 1.2 × 1.2m/4 × 4ft

Rosa 'Mundi' (*Rosa gallica versicolor*) Pale rosy-pink blotched and striped with cerise-pink. Very fragrant. 1.2 × 1.2m/4 × 4ft

◆ *Rosa 'Mundi' is often grown as a hedge.*

'Charles de Mills' The 'sliced off' appearance shows the petals remarkably whorled and quartered. 1.5 × 1.2m/5 × 4ft

It is lore that any shoot bearing seven leaves is a 'sucker'. Most shrub roses have seven leaves. 'Suckers' are normally quite easily distinguishable.

Gallicas often spread themselves monopodially underground – in time, one bush can form into a substantial thicket. These are not 'suckers'.

Die unto themselves sweet Roses do not so, Of their sweet deaths are the sweetest odours made. (Rosa gallica officinalis) Shakespeare.

'Empress Josephine' (*Rosa × francofurtana*) Deeply veined grey-green foliage and smooth stems, bearing rose-pink blooms, veined and flushed with mauve, followed by turbinate hips. 1 × 1.2m/3 × 4ft

GALLICA ROSES

Never replace old rose beds with new roses without excavating and changing 45cm/1½ft depth of soil, or else rest it for three years.

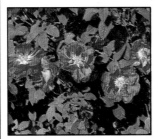

Rosa gallica officinalis ('The Apothecary's Rose', 'Red Rose of Lancaster'). Very fragrant. 1.2 × 1.2m/ 4 × 4ft

'Camaieux' Striking semi-double loosely formed white flowers striped and splashed with crimson and purple. 1.5 × 1m/5 × 3ft

'Tuscany Superb' Large, full, semi-double blooms of intense dark crimson-maroon fading to violet-maroon. 1.5 × 1m/5 × 3ft

'Président de Sèze' ('Jenny Duval') Striking two-toned, fully double blooms, of dark magenta-crimson in the centre, paling to lilac-white round the edges. 1.5m × 90cm/5 × 3ft

◆ *Flowering branches may need staking to support the weight of blooms.*

ROSA DAMASCENA, OFFSPRING OF *ROSA GALLICA* AND *ROSA PHOENICIA*.
Introduced from Damascus by the Crusaders, Damasks were cultivated, by the Romans, principally for the production of attar of roses (rose oil). For this they remain famous today. Sturdy shrubs, with bristly, thorny stems and deeply veined, downy grey-green leaves, bearing large double, loose clusters of fragrant flowers in hues of pink and white.

'Madame Zoetmans' Densely petalled, usually quartered flowers with a central green button. 1.2 × 1m/4 × 3ft

DAMASK ROSES

Kazanlük in Bulgaria is renowned for its otto or attar of roses. It takes 4kg of blooms to produce 1gm of rose oil.

Damask roses make wonderful floriferous hedges as well as providing form to a planting of perennials. They may be trimmed to shape.

'Léda' (The Painted Damask) Reddish-brown buds opening to milky-white blooms suffused with blush-pink – unmistakably marked with carmine tones. Beautifully scented. 1 × 1m/3 × 3ft

◆ *'Léda' makes a good sturdy bush with very dark green leaves.*

DAMASK
ROSES

'Gloire de Guilan' Highly fragrant fully double, flat quartered blooms. Light green foliage and numerous thorns. 1.2 × 1.2m/4 × 4ft

◆ *This sprawling rose is grown for producing attar of roses.*

'Ispahan' ('Pompon des Princes') Pretty clusters on a fine bushy shrub. Creates a long and brilliant display. 1.5 × 1.2m/5 × 4ft

'Madame Hardy' blushed flesh-pink at first – opening to pure white. 1.5 × 1.5m/5 × 5ft

◆ *The cupped flowers reflex to reveal a green button eye.*

'Kazanlük' ('Trigintipetala') Grown for attar of roses and potpourri. Pale apple-green foliage, very fragrant flowers. 2 × 2m/6 × 6ft

'La Ville de Bruxelles' Fine luxuriant light green foliage and strong upright growth. Strong fragrance. 1.5 × 1m/5 × 3ft

'Celsiana' Pretty clusters of large semi-double pinky-white flowers. Very fragrant. 1.5 × 1.2m/5 × 4ft

'York and Lancaster' (*Rosa damascena versicolor*) Loosely formed semi-double flowers amid downy grey-green leaves. 2 × 2m/6 × 6ft

THE WHITE ROSES OF HISTORICAL IMPORTANCE, dating back to the Middle Ages. Handsome grey-green foliage, stems and hips. Tolerance of semi-shade and poor soil divulge the Dog rose as one parent; and the sweetly scented, tightly packed, very double blooms, in shades of pale pink and white are characteristic of *Rosa damascena*, the other. Remarkably versatile, as trained or specimen shrubs.

'Königin von Dänemark' ('Queen of Denmark') Carmine tinted buds opening to large, fragrant, distinctly quartered, pale-pink flowers with button centre. Dark blue-green foliage. 1.5 × 1.2m/5 × 4ft

'Alba semi-plena' Cluster of semi-double milky-white blooms with prominent golden stamens. Effective grey-green foliage. Round red hips in autumn. Very fragrant. 2 × 1.5m/6 × 5ft

'Great Maiden's Blush' ('Cuisse de Nymphe') Pale blush-pink, semi-double flowers with muddled centres, amid ample lush grey-green foliage. Strong sweet fragrance. 1.5 × 1.2m/5 × 4ft

Thorough soil preparation prior to planting is essential for establishing a good root system of any rose – even if it is 'tolerant of poor soil'.

Albas tolerate semi-shade; as in woodland plantings, where some varieties may be trained to climb into trees. No rose thrives in dense shade.

171

ALBA ROSES

'Alba Maxima' Fully double slightly blushed flowers with muddled centres. Very fragrant. 2 × 1.5m/6 × 5ft

◆ *Also known as 'The Jacobite Rose' or 'White Rose of York'.*

'Félicité Parmentier' Unusually short for an Alba. Fresh-pink quartered blooms with button eye. 1.2 × 1.2m/4 × 4ft

'Celestial' ('Céleste') Rosy-pink buds opening to clear pale pink, semi-double flowers. Very scented. 2 × 1.5m/6 × 5ft

◆ *Perfectly scrolled buds make this a good cutting rose.*

'Madame Legras de St. Germain' Deliciously scented, slightly cupped, well filled blooms of glistening ivory-white flushed yellow. Graceful arching growth which may be trained to climb. 2 × 1.2m/6 × 4ft

ALSO KNOWN AS 'CABBAGE ROSES', as well as the 'Hundred-Leaved rose', hence the name Centifolia. Centifolias are notable for their distinctive flowers and foliage which scale precisely in accordance with the size of the shrub, ranging from large to miniature. The blooms are large, heavy and globular, reflexing to reveal the famous quartered centre and green button eye.

CENTIFOLIA ROSES

Rosa centifolia ('The Provence Rose', 'The Cabbage Rose') Large, clear-pink flowers. 2 × 1.5m/6 × 5ft

'Pompon de Bourgogne' ('Parvifolia', 'Burgundy Rose') A miniature bushy shrub bearing rosette-type flowers. 1m × 60cm/3 × 2ft

'Chapeau de Napoléon' ('Cristata', 'Napoleon's Hat', 'Crested Moss') Beautiful blooms with winged calyx. 1.5 × 1.2m/5 × 4ft

'Fantin Latour' Fragrant cupped flowers, packed with blush-pink petals deepening towards the centre – classically quartered with button eye. Later the outer petals reflex. 2 × 1.5m/6 × 5ft

'De Meaux' A short bushy shrub of fastigiate habit, bearing miniature Centifolia-type, pale grey-green foliage and tiny pink flat rosette-shaped flowers. 1 × 1m/3 × 3ft

◆ *This rose is very prone to black spot.*

CENTIFOLIA ROSES

The tall varieties are open and lax requiring some support while the miniatures are bushy and compact enough to be grown in a pot.

After flowering reduce long canes by one third or more. All dead and twiggy wood should be removed. Trim miniature varieties hard.

Rosa centifolia, also known as 'The Provence Rose' – its superb flower forms are often depicted in paintings, thus the name 'Rose des Peintres'.

Above from left to right: 'Ombrée Parfaite', 'Juno', 'Robert le Diable', 'Chapeau de Napoléon', 'Fantin Latour'. Huge heavy globular opulent blooms containing one hundred petals.

'Petite de Hollande'
('Pompon des Dames')
Beautiful, fragrant flowers.
1.2 × 1m/4 × 3ft

◆ *'Petite de Hollande' makes a compact leafy shrub.*

'Spong' Miniature, cupped, rich-pink flowers – slightly larger than 'Rose de Meaux', opening flat on a compact upright shrub with rounded grey-green leaves. $1.2 \times 1m/4 \times 3ft$

MOSS ROSES

ROSA CENTIFOLIA MUSCOSA. Developed from a mossy mutation or sport of *Rosa centifolia*. Moss roses added novelty to rose breeding, concentrating innovations towards richly colourful, luxuriantly textured, resin-scented, mossy growths round the calyxes and stems. Not to the detriment of the blooms – which with their rich tones and deep fragrance took on a new exotic appearance! Often repeat-flowering.

The buds of Moss roses are covered in numerous variants of fascinating resinous moss. They open slowly, revealing richly colourful, deeply fragrant blooms.

'Blanche Moreau' A vigorous, slender, somewhat lax shrub.. Often recurrent. 2 × 1.2m/6 × 4ft

'Madame Delaroche-Lambert' Brownish-green mossy buds opening to fragrant, crimson-purple, flattish flowers with rolled outer petals and muddled centres. Dark healthy foliage. Repeats well. 1.2 × 1.2m/4 × 4ft

'Gloire des Mousseux' ('Madame Alboni') Enormous full-petalled blooms of clear bright pink. 1.2 × 1m/4 × 3ft

◆ Buds are lightly mossed amid plentiful light green foliage.

'Capitaine John Ingram' Tightly packed, slightly mossy buds opening to flat, compact, pompon-shaped blooms. 1.2 × 1m/4 × 3ft

MOSS ROSES

'Proliferation' is when the vegetative part of a bud develops from inside-out, resulting in severe malformation. It can be caused by extreme temperature fluctuations.

Don't fork round the roots of a rose – carefully apply herbicide to rid perennial weeds and maintain a generous mulch.

'Alfred de Dalmas' ('Mousseline') Sweetly scented creamy-white tinged pink, loosely formed blooms. A compact twiggy bush. 1.2 × 1.2m/4 × 4ft

◆ *'Alfred de Dalmas' flowers freely from midsummer to autumn.*

'Général Kléber' Soft bright green mossy buds opening to informal, double shining blooms, very fragrant, in soft pure pink, amid ample bright fresh foliage. 1.2 × 1.2m/4 × 4ft

'Henri Martin' Makes a tall graceful shrub. Clusters of small, tightly packed, clear-crimson flowers. Fairly fragrant. 1.5 × 1.2m/5 × 4ft

'Louis Gimard' Dark, mossy, densely packed buds opening to large flat blooms with muddled centres. Very fragrant. 1.5 × 1m/5 × 3ft

'William Lobb' ('Old Velvet Moss') Large clusters of blooms which fade to lavender-grey tinted with white. 2.4 × 1.5m/8 × 5ft

3. OLD SHRUB ROSES (REPEAT FLOWERING)

Cherished in small gardens today for their distinction and flexibility.

CHINA ROSES

VIGOROUS, BUSHY, SOMEWHAT TWIGGY SHRUBS, which will flower continuously all summer, and often longer when positioned in a sheltered spot. Despite the fragile appearance of the exquisite flowers (in a mouth-watering range of hues) and dainty foliage, the shrubs are extremely hardy and very versatile. They may be pruned hard, trained against a wall or allowed to scrabble randomly.

China roses are surprisingly tough and vigorous, flowering continuously all summer. Many are capable of climbing to a considerable height.

'Old Blush China' is often seen blooming on Christmas day. Hellebores are the other 'Christmas roses'.

'Viridiflora' ('The Green Rose') The petals and sepals apparently merge – green tinged with brown! A vigorous upright free-flowering shrub popular for flower arrangements. Odd peppery fragrance.
1 × 1m/3 × 3ft

'Old Blush China' ('Parson's Pink China', 'The Monthly Rose') Clusters of delicate lilac-pink sweetly scented flowers on a dainty twiggy shrub. 1.2 × 1m/ 4 × 3ft

'Irene Watts' Salmony-pink pointed buds open to full, flat, loosely double flowers. Very free-flowering. Bushy dark green purple-tinted foliage. 60 × 60cm/2 × 2ft

'Hermosa' Small cupped lilac-pink blooms produced continuously throughout the season. 1 × 1m/3 × 3ft

'Mutabilis' ('Tipo Ideale', *Rosa turkestana*) Single papery flowers borne on delicate airy panicles. 1.2 × 1m/4 × 3ft

'Bloomfield Abundance' Miniature blooms borne at the tips of huge airy panicles. Upright wiry growth. 2 × 1.2m/6 × 4ft

'Sophie's Perpetual' Sprays of shapely, double, silvery-pink globe-shaped blooms. Sweetly scented. 2 × 1.2m/6 × 4ft

◆ *A twiggy shrub with healthy dark green foliage.*

AUTUMN DAMASK ROSES

The other name for these roses is Portland roses.

REMARKABLE FOR THEIR ABILITY TO FLOWER INTERMITTENTLY from midsummer until autumn, greatly extending the rose season. Shorter and more compact than the Damasks; the stronger tones, very double flowers and rich fragrance are among the main virtues of these very useful shrubs in today's gardens. They were acclaimed after 1800 but were superseded in cultivation and popularity by the Hybrid Perpetuals.

'Portland Rose' Prolific bright crimson, semi-double, fragrant blooms, displaying bright golden stamens. Vigorous and sturdy growth with excellent mid-green foliage. 60 × 60cm/2 × 2ft

◆ *If dead blooms are removed, the 'Portland Rose' will remain in flower from midsummer until autumn.*

'Rose du Roi' (*Rosa paestana*, 'Scarlet Four Seasons') Parent of the Hybrid perpetuals. Large, fragrant, very double bright crimson-red flowers on a sturdy vigorous shrub.
1 × 1m/3 × 3ft

'Rose de Rescht' Small, neat, extremely fragrant, glowing-crimson lightening to magenta, pompon-shaped flowers. Short bushy shrub with dark purplish-green foliage.
1 × 1m/3 × 3ft

◆ *The beautiful quartering of these blooms which are borne from midsummer until autumn make this rose well worth growing.*

'Comte de Chambord' Large globular buds opening to very fragrant full flat quartered lilac-pink blooms. Forms a nice upright shrub if kept pruned. 1.2m × 1m/4 × 3ft

'Jacques Cartier' A vigorous yet short and compact bush. Delicious fragrance.
1.2 × 1m/4 × 3ft

◆ *'Jacques Cartier' is a very reliable repeat flowerer.*

'Quatre Saisons' (*Rosa damascena bifera*, 'The Rose of Four Seasons') Parent of the Bourbon roses.
1.5 × 1.5m/5 × 5ft

Shorter and more compact than the Damasks, Damask Perpetuals make excellent hedges; some varieties grow well in a pot.

If roses show signs of potassium deficiency, banana skins may be your answer! Strewn beneath the mulch, roses rapidly absorb this valuable source of potassium.

BOURBON ROSES

Bourbons require good pruning to succeed. In winter reduce long canes by one third, and cut side-shoots back to three eyes ('spur pruning').

'Boule de Neige' Clusters of sweetly scented, quartered blooms which reflex into a ball. 1.2 × 1m/4 × 3ft

'Souvenir de la Malmaison' Soft flesh-pink cups opening to huge, regularly quartered, sweetly fragrant blooms. 1 × 1m/3 × 3ft

'Souvenir de Saint Anne's' Very fragrant flowers in perfect formation amid good foliage. 2 × 1.5m/6 × 5ft

'Louise Odier' Perfectly assembled cup-shaped blooms. Very perpetual and fragrant. 1.5 × 1.2m/5 × 4ft

'Madame Isaac Pereire' Enormous, cupped and quartered blooms amid abundant, dark foliage. 2 × 1.5m/ 6 × 5ft

◆ *This rose may be trained to climb.*

'Madame Pierre Oger' A short, bushy sport of 'Reine Victoria'. Very pale blooms intensify in sunny weather. 1.2 × 1.2m/4 × 4ft

IN 1817 A CHANCE SEEDLING WAS DISCOVERED on the Isle de Bourbon east of Madagascar – probably a cross between the two cultivars 'Quatre Saisons' and 'Old Blush China', commonly used as hedging. By intercrossing it with Gallicas and Damasks the Bourbons developed. The flowers are round and full-petalled, richly fragrant in bold tones and stripes and appear intermittently all summer, some of their finest blooms borne in late summer. Dead-head and feed, following the first burst of bloom.

'Reine Victoria' A tall slender shrub bearing soft, cupped blooms. Very fragrant and perpetual. 2 × 1m/6 × 3ft

'Honorine de Brabant' Very vigorous with handsome light green foliage. 2 × 1.5m/6 × 5ft

'Variegata di Bologna' Strong arching growth bearing spectacular, fragrant, fully cupped, double flowers. 1.5 × 1.2m/5 × 4ft

◆ *'Variegata di Bologna' is also a strong climber.*

HYBRID PERPETUAL ROSES

DESCENDANTS OF AUTUMN DAMASKS, BOURBONS AND CHINAS, predecessors of Hybrid Teas. Popular with Victorians who enjoyed them pegged down in beds, trained up pillars, floated in water and worn in their hair! Ranging from short bushes to tall lax shrubs, the flowers are full, richly perfumed in gorgeous hues of maroon, purple, crimson and violet, in successive crops throughout the summer.

'Baron Girod de L'Ain'
Bright crimson-red flowers with marked white edging to each petal. The flower-form is cupped in the centre, reflexed at the edges. 1.5 × 1.2m/5 × 4ft

'Général Jacqueminot' A vigorous shrub with Damask fragrance and abundant fresh-green foliage. 1.5 × 1.2m/5 × 4ft

'Hugh Dickson' Perfumed and free-flowering, it produces such long shoots it could almost be treated as a climber. 2.4 × 1.5m/8 × 5ft

Right: **'Baroness Rothschild'** at the centre of a selection of rich Hybrid Perpetuals, including **'Souvenir du Docteur Jamain'** (top left), **'Gloire de Ducher'** (top right), **'Ferdinand Pichard'** (bottom right) and **'Roger Lambelin'** (bottom left). Planting Hybrid Perpetuals in a border is a real opportunity for the artist's palette, in gorgeous hues of maroon, crimson and pink which co-ordinate on a par with asters.

'Frau Karl Druschki' ('Snow Queen') Pink-tinted buds opening to large pure-white flowers with notable high lemon-tinted centres. Light green foliage. Vigorous erect growth. 1.5 × 1m/5 × 3ft

'Reine des Violettes' Grape-purple fading to warm parma-violet. Vigorous growth, few thorns. 1.5 × 1m/5 × 3ft

'Ulrich Brunner Fils' Vigorous upright habit with luxuriant foliage. Deeply fragrant. 2.2 × 1.2m/7 × 4ft

4. MODERN SHRUB ROSES

Relatively recent introductions – an outstandingly useful collection of shrubs which range from the giant and arching to the dwarf and cushion-like.

HYBRID SPECIES ROSES

'Frühlingsgold' Masses of large, semi-double, pale-yellow flowers, deepening towards a showy golden boss, smother a luxuriantly foliated shrub. Very fragrant. 2.2 × 2m/7 × 6ft

'Frühlingsmorgen' A single, free-flowering rose of more compact growth than 'Frühlingsgold'. 2 × 1.5m/6 × 5ft

'Anna Zinkeisen' Clusters of fragrant, fully double reflexing flowers. Prolific light-green glossy foliage. 1.2 × 1.2m/4 × 4ft

'Gipsy Boy' ('Zigeunerknabe') Tolerates poor soil and part shade. Summer flowering. 1.5 × 1.2m/5 × 4ft

'Nevada' Fragrant flowers in profusion along arching stems. 2.4 × 2.2m/8 × 7ft

'Cerise Bouquet' Medium-sized, cerise-pink flowers, borne in sprays along arching stems. 2.7 × 2.7m/9 × 9ft

'Maigold' Vigorous prickly arching growth with bright glossy foliage. Good as a climber. 1.5 × 2.4m/5 × 8ft

'Robbie Burns' Single, cupped, delicately fragrant flowers. Round black hips follow. 1.5 × 1.5m/5 × 5ft

'Fritz Nobis' A very vigorous shrub with glossy dark green foliage. Summer flowering. Good hips. 1.5 × 1.2m/5 × 4ft

'Marguerite Hilling' Warm rich-pink flowers contrast nicely with dark chocolate stems. 2.4 × 2.2m/8 × 7ft

'Scharlachglut' ('Scarlet Fire') Large, single flowers. Deep-red stems, arching growth. Large bottle-shaped hips. 2.2 × 2m/7 × 6ft

THESE ARE THE GIANTS OF MODERN SHRUB ROSES, very closely related to the Species roses. The flowers, reminiscent of the Dog roses, are brighter, larger and more double, giving a magnificent display in early summer often repeating in late summer. The shrubs are tough and are suitable as specimens, planted singly or in groups; as hedging and as screening.

HYBRID SPECIES ROSES

'Constance Spry' Large double, clear luminous-pink, globular blooms in profusion on a spectacular lax-growing shrub. Requires some support. Summer flowering. 2.4 × 2m/8 × 6ft

◆ *'Constance Spry' is a spectacular sight in midsummer trained as a climber, over a wall, fence or trellis.*

DWARF POLYANTHA ROSES

The other name for these roses is Poly-pom roses.

LOW-GROWING BUSHES UNRIVALLED FOR USEFULNESS, VIGOUR AND HEALTH, flowering continuously from midsummer until autumn. Clusters of exquisite fragrant flowers in shades of pink, lemon and white, mostly in small pompons or rosettes. Ideally suited for mixed borders, planted in groups amongst perennials and shrubs, and for carpeting beneath standard roses. Also suitable for pots.

'Nathalie Nypels' Prolific, semi-double, bright pinky-white flowers with lemony stamens, on a vigorous but low, spreading bush. Healthy dark foliage. Very fragrant. 1 × 1m/3 × 3ft

'Francine Austin' Low arching growth with twiggy stems bearing dainty sprays of small, glistening-white pompons. 1 × 1.2m/3 × 4ft

◆ *This is a healthy and continuous bloomer.*

'Yvonne Rabier' Clusters of small, double, pure-white flowers against dark, glossy, healthy foliage. 1.2 × 1m/ 4 × 3ft

'The Fairy' Massive sprays of perfectly formed small pale-pink rosettes. Delicate fragrance. 60cm × 1m/2 × 3ft

◆ *This rose makes a short, dense, spreading bush.*

Dwarf Polyantha or Poly-pom roses, sadly, have little fragrance, but grouped or mass-planted, their effect is unsurpassed for continuity of flower.

'Little White Pet' Perpetual flowering, panicles of small, white, double rosettes, pink in bud, amid dark foliage. 60 × 60cm/2 × 2ft

◆ *This rose is a dwarf sport of 'Félicité et Perpétue'.*

'Cécile Brunner' ('The Sweetheart Rose') Miniature shell-pink Hybrid Tea shaped blooms. Sweet scent. 1m × 60cm/3 × 2ft

'Perle d'Or' ('Yellow Cécile Brunner') Small, softly fragrant flowers on a short twiggy bush. 1m × 60cm/ 3 × 2ft

'Ballerina' Flowers borne in large, prolific corymbs, like those of a hydrangea. 1.2 × 1m/4 × 3ft

◆ *'Ballerina' makes a good miniature or half-standard rose for a pot.*

193

HYBRID MUSK ROSES

ROSA MOSCHATA HYBRIDS. Deliciously fragrant flowers in compatible shades of cream, pink, yellow and scarlet, in small clusters at midsummer, but producing magnificent, long panicles throughout late summer and autumn. Dark reddish-brown young stems and handsome foliage. Equally at home in a bed of their own, mixed border, as a hedge or trained over a trellis or fence.

'Sally Holmes' Single flowers, borne in enormous corymbs. Vigorous erect habit. Large healthy foliage. 1.5 × 1.2m/5 × 4ft

'Prosperity' Clusters of pinky-tinged buds opening to deliciously scented, ivory-white flowers tinted yellow at the centre. May be trained to climb. 1.5 × 1.2m/5 × 4ft

'Buff Beauty' Large trusses of fully double, warm apricot blooms. 1.5 × 1.5m/5 × 5ft

◆ *'Buff Beauty' may be trained to climb.*

'Moonlight' Enormous trusses of white flowers against dark foliage. Musk-rose fragrance. 1.5 × 1.2m/ 5 × 4ft

'Felicia' Large trusses bearing warm-pink buds tinted with apricot opening to silvery-pink semi-double flowers. Vigorous upright growth. Dark glossy foliage. 1.5 × 1.5m/5 × 5ft

'Penelope' Salmony-orange buds opening to semi-double blooms of creamy-pink, turning to white. Rich musk fragrance. 2 × 1.2m/6 × 4ft

◆ *'Penelope' produces beautiful cool-green, bloom-covered hips.*

A small garden of hybrid musks with peonies and other herbaceous planting.

'Cornelia' Large sprays bearing rich copper-tinted buds opening to small rosettes of salmon-pink turning to creamy-pink. May be trained to climb. 1.5 × 1.5m/5 × 5ft

◆ *It pays to remove the unsightly dead-heads of 'Cornelia'.*

ENGLISH ROSES

RELATIVELY RECENT INTRODUCTIONS with the unique charm reminiscent of Old roses having typical rosette or full-cupped, globular flowers and powerful individual fragrance. This is combined with repeat-flowering and the more compact habit of Modern Bush roses. The characterful flowers predominate over the non-distinctive but good, bushy habit, enlivening the limited range of cream, yellow, apricot and red hues.

'Perdita' Perfectly quartered flowers in deep cups of delicate creamy-apricot blushed with pink. Deep-green disease resistant foliage. Charming slightly lax habit. 1 × 1m/3 × 3ft

'Charles Austin' Large cupped full-petalled blooms with rich fruity fragrance. Vigorous upright growth which is excellent for cutting. 1.5 × 1.2m/5 × 4ft

'Graham Thomas' Fully double, softly cupped blooms, light green healthy foliage. 1.2 × 1.2m/4 × 4ft

'Sweet Juliet' Shallow cupped and quartered flowers. Strong leafy upright growth. Very fragrant. 1.2 × 1m/4 × 3ft

'The Pilgrim' Soft yellow rosettes on a very robust free-flowering bush with shiny green leaves. 1.1 × 1m/3½ × 3ft

'Cymbeline' Cool grey-blush flowers with a powerful myrrh fragrance on strong arching growth. 1.2 × 1.5m/4 × 5ft

'Symphony' Sweetly fragrant blooms amid plentiful medium-green foliage. Short bushy habit. 1 × 1m/3 × 3ft

'Lucetta' Strong arching growth bearing healthy dark foliage and semi-double flowers. 1.2 × 1.2m/4 × 4ft

'Charles Rennie Mackintosh' Tough, vigorous and bushy with fragrant flowers.
1m × 75cm/3 × 2½ft

'Sharifa Asma' Cupped at first, reflexing into deeply fragrant rosettes. Short, upright growth.
1m × 60cm/3 × 2ft

'Mary Rose' A good disease-resistant shrub with bright loosely formed flowers, only slighted scented. 1.2 × 1.2m/4 × 4ft

The tendency to arch to the ground under the weight of the blooms is overcome by reducing canes by one half or more in winter.

'Heritage' Vigorous bushy habit bearing huge round, cupped blooms. Marvellous strong fragrance.
1.2 × 1.2m/4 × 4ft

'Prospero' A perfect rosette of rich deep crimson turning to purple. Low spreading shrub.
60cm × 1m/2 × 3ft

'Chianti' Gallica-type rosettes. Richly perfumed. Summer flowering.
1.5 × 1.5m/5 × 5ft

'L.D. Braithwaite' Blooms freely produced over a long period of time. Lovely 'Old rose' fragrance. Unaffected by rain. 1.2 × 1.2m/4 × 4ft

'Gertrude Jekyll' Pretty buds opening to large fragrant blooms.
1.2 × 1m/4 × 3ft

◆ *Upright, robust and very healthy foliage.*

GROUND-COVER ROSES

THE VICTORIANS USED ROSES AS BEDDING. Modern landscapers have given breeders a similar specification but emphasize low-maintenance as the priority. Ground-cover roses range from huge trailing sprawlers which can smother and transform dull banks, to low-growing, compact shrubs, forming mounds of brightness and texture; and miniature carpeters which hug the sides of pots!

'Raubritter' Low trailing mounds bearing clusters of semi-double very cupped lilac-pink flowers in profusion. Attractive greyish foliage. Slight fragrance. Summer flowering. 1 × 1.5m/3 × 5ft

'Paulii' Vigorous thorny shoots form a dense, low, spreading mound. Large single pure-white papery flowers with crinkled petals, scented of cloves. Summer flowering. 1 × 2.7m/3 × 9ft

'Red Max Graf' Low and spreading, bushy shrub. Bright coppery-green, glossy foliage. Flowers midsummer onwards. 60cm × 1.5m/2 × 5ft

'Red Blanket' Scarlet-red flowers all summer with excellent shiny disease-resistant foliage. 1.2 × 1.5m/4 × 5ft

'Pink Bells' Rich-pink pompons borne in sprays amid small dark glossy healthy foliage. Forms a cushion. Flowers midsummer onwards. 60cm × 1.2m/2 × 4ft

'Rosy Cushion' Very similar in habit to 'Red Blanket'. Flowers continuously all summer. 1.2 × 1.5m/4 × 5ft

Descending the steps: **'Red Max Graf'**, *Verbascum chaixii* 'Album', 'Pink Bells', *Eremurus robustus* 'Alba', **'Raubritter'**, **'Rosy Cushion'**, **'Snow Carpet'**, *Bergenia* 'Admiral' form carpets, cascades and cushions, smothering the side of the steps and climbing into a steep bank emphasized by occasional spiky perennials.

5. CLIMBING ROSES

Climbing roses all have one thing in common – they climb! But their flower-shapes, scent, climbing habit and vigorousness are largely in accordance with their parentage.

CLIMBING NOISETTE ROSES

'Alister Stella Grey'
('Golden Rambler') Small clusters – increasing as summer goes on – of loosely formed, fragrant yellow flowers with dark centres. Also good as a shrub. 5 × 3m/16 × 10ft

'Gloire de Dijon' ('The Old Glory Rose') Very large, extremely fragrant, full-cupped and quartered flowers of buffy pinky-apricot tones. Vigorous leafy growth. Tolerates part shade. 3.5 × 2.4m/12 × 8ft

'Madame Alfred Carrière'
Prolific clusters of large, informally double, fragrant, white tinged with pink blooms. Vigorous, fairly thorn-free, light green foliage. Tolerates partial shade. 3.5 × 3m/12 × 10ft

'Goldfinch' Large tightly-packed clusters of small semi-double flowers – golden-yellow on opening turning to cream with dark orange stamens. Summer flowering. 3 × 2m/10 × 6ft

'Meg' Beautiful, large, open semi-double flowers. 3.5 × 2m/12 × 6ft

◆ *Meg's dark glossy foliage is a good setting for the delicate blooms.*

'Cécile Brunner' A vigorous climber with tiny Hybrid Tea-shaped blooms. 5 × 3m/16 × 10ft

BRED FROM AN ORIGINAL CROSS between 'Parson's Pink China' and *Rosa moschata*, which was brought to France from America in the 1800s: prolific clusters of highly fragrant rosette-type flowers in delicate shades of pink, yellow and white.

CLIMBING NOISETTE ROSES

'Blush Noisette' The original Noisette rose. Clusters of medium-sized prettily cupped, pinky-white flowers. Sweetly scented of cloves. Very continuous. Also good as a shrub. 2.2 × 1.2m/7 × 4ft

◆ *Climbing Noisettes flower mostly from summer until autumn, thriving on a sunny wall, trellis, arch or pergola – protected from frost and cold winds.*

Large-Flowered Climbing Roses

DERIVATIVES OF MANY FAVOURITES IN THE BOOK – WHICH CAN CLIMB. They all bear large fragrant, conspicuous flowers in an exciting range of shapes, formations and colours. An eye-catching spectacle trained up a wall, pillar, fence or trellis; some varieties tolerant of shady aspects; most performing repeat displays throughout summer and often into autumn. Large-flowered climbing roses are often climbing versions or 'sports' of Bush roses. Distinguishable from other climbing roses by their large, bright blooms.

'Madame Grégoire Staechelin' ('Spanish Beauty') Summer flowering. 5 × 3m/16 × 10ft

'Zéphirine Drouhin' (Bourbon) Flowers borne on thornless stems. Tolerates part shade. 3 × 2m/10 × 6ft

'Dortmund' Clusters of single blooms – followed by hips. 2.4 × 2m/8 × 6ft

◆ *'Dortmund' is good as a hedge.*

'Blairii Number Two' (Bourbon) Large, fragrant, globular very double blooms. 3.5 × 2m/12 × 6ft

'Aloha' Fully petalled blooms on strong upright growth with dark leathery foliage. Very fragrant. 3 × 1.5m/10 × 5ft

'Lady Hillingdon'
(Climbing Tea) Large, rich
apricot-yellow blooms which
hang their heads.
3.5 × 2.4m/12 × 8ft

'Alchemist' Large full
rosette-shaped flowers.
Summer flowering. 3.5 ×
2.4m/12 × 8ft

'Mermaid' Large, single,
sulphur-yellow flowers with
deep amber stamens.
Vigorous growth.
8 × 3.5m/26 × 12ft

◆ *'Mermaid' requires a
high wall sheltered from
cold winds.*

LARGE-FLOWERED CLIMBING ROSES

'Compassion' Typical
Hybrid Tea-shaped flowers.
Vigorous upright growth
bearing dark stems and
dark glossy healthy foliage.
3 × 2m/10 × 6ft

'Leverkusen' A vigorous
shrub or climber. Mid-green
glossy, serrated foliage, with
clusters of medium sized,
loosely-double, lemon-
yellow, sweetly fragrant
flowers. 3 × 2m/10 × 6ft

'New Dawn' Fragrant
flowers amid healthy glossy
dark foliage. Tolerates part
shade. 3.5 × 2.4m/12 × 8ft

'Souvenir de la Malmaison'
(Bourbon). Flowers twice: in
midsummer and late
summer. 3.5 × 2.4m/12 × 8ft

'Sombreuil' (Tea Climber)
Fully double flat, quartered
blooms. Delicious Tea scent.
Ample lush-green foliage.
2.4 × 1.5m/8 × 5ft

RAMBLER ROSES

EXTREMELY VIGOROUS CREEPING GROWTH, bearing huge trusses of small flowers in a prolific display during early to midsummer – filling the air with fragrance, sometimes repeating late summer. Unrivalled floriferous coverage for pillars, arches, pergolas, arbours and fences, intensified when combined with Noisettes, Large-flowered climbers and clematis. The most vigorous varieties may be trained up into trees.

When the main flush of (from left to right) **'Léontine Gervais'**, **'Félicité et Perpétue'**, **'Violette'** is over, the *Clematis* 'Jackmanii Superba' bridges the gap until **'Aimée Vibert'** and **'Cécile Brunner'** arrive for late summer.

'Albéric Barbier'
(Wichuraiana) Yellow buds opening to fully double creamy-white fragrant flowers with almost evergreen, ample glossy foliage. Repeats in late summer. 5 × 3m/16 × 10ft

Arches, pergolas and trellis divide the space and create rooms and walkways. They quickly make a garden three-dimensional and interesting.

Don't cut back new growth on Ramblers – they may never have flowers! It is these new growths which bear the flowers the following season.

'Bobbie James' (Multiflora) Exceptionally large corymbs bearing sweetly scented, creamy-white, semi-double flowers. Makes massive growth with its abundant light green foliage. $10 \times 7\text{m}/33 \times 23\text{ft}$

'Francis E. Lester' (Moschata hybrid) Huge fragrant clusters of neat single flowers – pink in bud, opening to pinky-white, followed by small orange-red hips. $5 \times 3\text{m}/16 \times 10\text{ft}$

'Paul's Himalayan Musk' (Moschata hybrid) Vigorous graceful growth bearing long trailing shoots and dainty hanging sprays of small double blush-pink rosettes. Very fragrant. $10 \times 7\text{m}/33 \times 23\text{ft}$

6. MODERN BUSH ROSES

Bush roses, compared to the intoxicating subtleties of Shrub roses, bring to the garden a palette of sharpened brightness. For this they should be exploited.

Hybrid Tea Roses

THE MOST POPULAR GARDEN ROSES OF THIS CENTURY. They followed after the Hybrid Perpetuals. Strong stems bearing large, solitary, upheld flowers, they demonstrate the exquisite variation in detail sought after by breeders in pursuit of the perfect bloom, encouraged by fashion and competition. Their rich satin-textured petals exemplify the multitude of hues. Suitable as bedding or border plants or for massed display.

'Simba' Exceptionally high-centred with very long petals – beautifully shaped in pure bright yellow. They appear dazzling against the abundant mid-green foliage.
75 × 75cm/2½ × 2½ft

'Just Joey' Fragrant blooms become extremely large in warm weather.
75 × 60cm/2½ × 2ft

'Ingrid Bergman' Large blooms borne on a strong upright free-flowering shrub. Good for cutting.
1m × 60cm/3 × 2ft

'Tequila Sunrise' Showy with a scarlet edging to its gold blooms. Glossy foliage.
75 × 75cm/2½ × 2½ft

'Doris Tysterman' Vigorous and upright in habit with bronze-green foliage. Slight fragrance.
1m × 75cm/3 × 2½ft

'Mrs Oakley Fisher' Graceful old single-flowered Hybrid Tea which is well scented. Bronze foliage.
1m × 1m/3 × 3ft

'Super Star' Flamboyant, for those who like brilliant colour. Fragrant. Branching growth. 1 × 1m/3 × 3ft

'Keepsake' Finely shaped glowing blooms, lightly scented. Upright and vigorous. Glossy leaves.
1 × 1m/3 × 3ft

'Alec's Red' Heavily scented and well formed blooms very freely produced. Dark glossy leaves. 1m × 75cm/3 × 2½ft

'Silver Jubilee' Elegant, finely formed flowers on a vigorous bush, well clothed with healthy foliage. 75 × 75cm/2½ × 2½ft

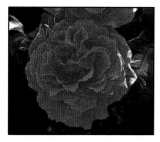

'Fragrant Cloud' Large perfumed flowers, very freely produced on a vigorous bush. 1 × 1m/3 × 3ft

'Royal William' Classic velvety blooms. Strong-necked, robust and healthy. 1 × 1m/3 × 3ft

◆ *One of the most fragrant of Modern Bush roses.*

211

FLORIBUNDA ROSES

Floribunda roses originated from a cross between a Hybrid Tea and a Polyantha rose in the 1920s. Their other name is Cluster-flowered roses.

THE FLOWERS OF FLORIBUNDAS ARE CARRIED IN CLUSTERS OR SPRAYS creating a vivid and often dramatic spectacle from early summer to autumn, particularly when planted in groups or in massed displays. Useful as border plants and as hedging. The smaller varieties may be grown in containers.

'Anne Harkness' Sprays of warm gold/apricot flowers. Healthy, could form a hedge. 1.2 × 1m/4 × 3ft

'Amber Queen' The rich amber is in harmony with the bronze-tinted leaves. 60 × 60cm/2 × 2ft

◆ *A very fragrant rose with spreading habit.*

'Mountbatten' Vigorous and shrubby with dark foliage and luminous double flowers. 1.2 × 1m/4 × 3ft

'City of Leeds' Reliable shrub with bronze-green foliage and freely produced clusters of blooms. 75 × 75cm/2½ × 2½ft

'Korresia' Very fragrant, long-lasting flowers on a compact bush. 75 × 75cm/2½ × 2½ft

'Matangi' One of the most vivid floribundas. Very flamboyant. Dark foliage. 75 × 75cm/2½ × 2½ft

'Sexy Rexy' Surprising name for a pretty double rose. Good bushy growth up to 1.2 × 1m/4 × 3ft

'Queen Elizabeth' The popular back-of-border or hedging rose. Strong and vigorous. 1.5 × 1m/5 × 3ft

'Escapade' Large single flowers like a wild rose, lilac to pink. Good mixer in a border. 1.2 × 1.2m/4 × 4ft

FLORIBUNDA ROSES

Liquid concentrated seaweed extract is excellent foliar feed. Add it to your fungicide and achieve two aims. Always spray when conditions are calm, preferably in the evening.

'Gruss an Aachen' Deep full cups in the Old rose style. Powerful fragrance. bushy upright growth. 60 × 60cm/2 × 2ft

'News' Large clusters of semi-double fullish blooms. Echoes its parent 'Tuscany Superb' (Gallica). 75 × 75cm/2½ × 2½ft

'Iceberg' The famous prolific white Floribunda, with pretty buds opening to wide double blossoms. 1.2 × 1.2m/4 × 4ft

◆ *'Iceberg' is a valuable bush rose for borders.*

Roses in unusual shades of copper, **'Edith Holden'** (in front), and pink with buff **'Iced Ginger'** (in the background), combine with perennials *Iris* 'Perryhill', the bright-scarlet spikes of *Penstemon barbatus* and ornamental grass *Ophiopogon planiscapus* 'Nigrescens'.

THE EARLY FLORIBUNDAS WERE IN PINKS AND REDS, then came the yellows. More recently the artist-breeder has dabbled with heavenly tones of apricot and copper and, on another note, revelled in ambiguous shades of lavender, mauve and brown! These innovations are curiosities on their own but can provide a source of inspiration for creating exciting planting schemes and flower arrangements.

FLORIBUNDA ROSES

'Lavender Pinocchio' A stunning little rose in both colour and form.
75 × 75cm/2½ × 2½ft

'Magenta' Clusters of 'Old Rose' rosettes in delicate shades of mauvish magenta-blue – the petals textured like porcelain. Fairly vigorous and fragrant.
1.5 × 1.2m/5 × 4ft

'Lilac Charm' An exquisite single flower in the palest lilac-mauve with prominent bushy red stamens borne on a compact bush with dark matt foliage.
60 × 60cm/2 × 2ft

'Brown Velvet' Russet-brown blooms borne freely amid bronze-green foliage.
75 × 60cm/2½ × 2ft

◆ *A good rose for flower arrangers.*

MINIATURE *and* PATIO ROSES

VERSATILITY IS AN INVALUABLE COMMODITY FOR ROSES in the modern small garden: be it patio, courtyard or balcony. The miniature, often rounded habit of these roses is ideally suited to forming neat, round cushions in paviour crevices and pots; also as low hedging and, where scale matters, in borders. The range of flower-shapes available in miniature form is extensive.

'City Lights' (Patio) Classically shaped blooms on a vigorous bush to 60cm/2ft

'The Valois Rose' (Patio) Double blooms, creamy yellow in bud deepening to carmine edges in maturity. 60cm/2ft

◆ *A vigorous, upright grower.*

'Perestroika' (Miniature) Little bright yellow blooms with reflexed petals cover bronze-green leaves. 45cm/1½ft

'Pretty Polly' (Miniature)
The bush has a rounded
habit, covered with
charming delicate blooms.
45cm/1½ft

'Gentle Touch' (Miniature)
Dainty flowers on a bushy
little shrub. 45cm/1½ft

'Sweet Dream' (Patio)
Upright growth, clustered
with very neat full-petalled
flowers with some scent.
45cm/1½ft

'Queen Mother' (Patio)
Rather like a miniature
Shrub rose – very strong
growing, good in a border
or pot. 75cm/2½ft

'Regensberg' (Patio) A
rounded bush smothered
with dramatic bright pink,
white-eyed flowers.
45cm/1½ft

'Sweet Magic' (Miniature)
Small neat gold and orange
blooms mass a well-foliaged
little bush to 45cm/1½ft.

'Scarlet Patio' (Patio)
Cluster of intensely
coloured flowers against
deep green glossy leaves.
Compact. 45cm/1½ft

'Snow Sunblaze'
(Miniature) Small very
double buds open into
reflexed blooms on this
little bush. 30cm/1ft

MINIATURE *and* PATIO ROSES

Miniature and Patio roses
provide a long and dazzling
display of colour and
interest, requiring less
maintenance than, say,
bedding annuals.

Hanging baskets and pots
are both suitable for
growing Miniature and
Patio roses. Train a dense
creeper to shade the roots
from drying out.

'Top Marks' (Miniature)
Small brilliant orange-
vermillion flowers and
glossy foliage. 45cm/1½ft
but shown here as a
standard.

217